D0880239

Say Hello to LIFE

What the Bible says about life after death

by
Rod
Huron

You may obtain a 64-page leader's guide to accompany this paperback. Order number 41033 from Standard Publishing or your local supplier.

A Division of Standard Publishing
Cincinnati, Ohio 45231
No. 41032

©1984 The STANDARD PUBLISHING CO., division of STANDEX INTERNATIONAL Corp.

Library of Congress Cataloging in Publication Data

Huron, Rod.
 Say hello to life.

 1. Future life—Biblical teaching.
2. Death—Biblical teaching. I. Title.
BS680.F83H87 1984   236'.2   85-2573
ISBN 0-87239-752-1

Printed in U.S.A.

1984

"... and free those who all their lives were held in slavery by their fear of death."

— Hebrews 2:15

Table of Contents

I have a rendezvous with death.
                    —Alan Seeger

Who Said Anything About Dying?

Who's talking about dying?
Are you sure it isn't you?
"If I flunk that test, I'm dead!"
"I'll just die if he doesn't ask me out this weekend!"
"I was so embarrassed I thought I'd die!"
"You kill me!"
Maybe you don't talk like that; maybe you do. Let's hope you didn't mean what you said about that test.

Sad to say, there are those who do mean it, and when life doesn't go their way they end it all. Every day more than a thousand young people in the United States try to kill themselves—and these are only the ones we know about.[1] Some experts believe that suicide is the number one killer of teenagers in this country.

Take a look at the funeral business. Nearly two million Americans died last year, and their families spent six and a half billion dollars to bury them, not to mention the cost of hospital beds, cars, planes, busses, trains, tractors, motorcycles, boats, and bicycles that figured in their dying, nor the guns, poisons, bridges, tall buildings, knives, narcotics, booze, and rope that brought others to the grave.

---

1. Mary Giffen, M.D., and Carol Felsenthal, "A Cry for Help: Teen Suicide," in *Family Circle*, March 8, 1983, p. 28.

There's money in dying.

Grown men buy land, smooth it over, dig in it, and sell the holes. They plant trees, reroute creeks, pour concrete, set up rigid marble benches so straight and hard a corpse wouldn't be caught dead on one, erect flagpoles, plant flowers, cut weeds, sow grass, construct roads, gates, toolsheds, and drafty chapels to echo the preacher's solemn words at the committal.

Investors buy stock in casket companies. Custom shops turn cars into limousines and hearses to transport the dead in comfort and bear the grieving family in stately grace.

Funeral flowers are big business, too. All those bucks don't come from prom orchids and Mother's Day geraniums.

Death comes in many forms.

When Jody Robinson, twenty-four, left home for her regular shift at the Holiday Inn, how could she know that a sixteen-year-old

---

Quit worrying.
You'll never see your death certificate.

---

would enter the lobby and push his way into her work space and stab her repeatedly until she lost consciousness, then steal two hundred dollars from the cash drawer? The assistant manager found her moments later, but she was dead before the paramedics could get there.

When was the first time you saw death? Was it when your puppy ran out in front of a car and was hit, and you ran up crying just in time to see its eyes glaze and feel the life go out of its little body?

Or was it when you were just a kid and you used to drop worms into the puddles out back and watch each worm writhe and twist until it finally sank lifeless to the bottom?

Who was the first person you ever saw dead? Was it your grandmother, lying in her casket in the funeral home, eyes shut and her glasses on?

Unless you're a nurse or have taken care of people who are really sick, you probably haven't seen someone actually die. But you've seen dead people, haven't you? On TV? Or when a child drowned in the neighborhood pool? Or after a bloody motorcycle accident? Or in a terrible automobile wreck?

I'll never forget the time our neighbor called us and said there had been an accident on the highway two blocks from where we lived.

Even though it was Sunday, my brother Jim and I wanted to go and see what had happened. Not often was there such an exciting event so close to home.

"We'll have time to go over and come back and still not be late for church," we told Mother.

So Jim and I went, Mother and Dad coming along with us.

We saw what we went there to look at. Two young men had spent most of the night drinking, then had started their car and had made it less than two miles when they came to a parked trailer-truck.

$KE = \frac{1}{2} Mv^2.$[2]

The human skull was not designed to withstand ramming the steel underframe of a semi-trailer at eighty miles per hour.

There wasn't much blood. Just a blunt hole in the one boy's forehead oozing brain tissue, and two awful staring eyes. The ambulance crew had already loaded the driver's body by the time we came onto the scene, so we saw only the boy in the passenger seat—what was left of it. And what was left of him.

We didn't stay long. Had to get ready for church, remember. I didn't get much out of the service, as I recall. All I could think of was that hole and those awful staring eyes.

Death in the Bible

The evening news shocks us with sudden, violent death. So does the Biblical record in Judges 19 with the account of the girl raped in Gibeah and left for dead, then her body horribly mutilated by the man she'd been living with.

Joab, one of David's officers, vented his hatred for Abner by stabbing him in the stomach, killing him (2 Samuel 3:26, 27). Later, Joab took a dagger to Amasa, spilling Amasa's intestines out onto the ground and leaving him wallowing in blood in the middle of the road. Someone else came along and dragged the body into a field and threw a garment over it.

Joab wasn't even there to see; he was after Sheba. Joab and his men pursued Sheba all the way to Abel Beth Maacah, laid siege to the place, and were battering down the wall when a woman from the town called out to him.

She asked Joab why he was trying to destroy her city. He told her he was after Sheba, and if they would hand over that person, he would call off his men.

---

2. Formula for Kinetic Energy (one-half times mass times speed to the second power).

"His head will be thrown to you from the wall," the woman answered.

And that's what happened. The people grabbed Sheba and held him down while they cut his head off, then carried it up to the wall and threw the thing down to Joab. Joab sounded the trumpet and his men withdrew (2 Samuel 20:9-22).

Jehu had Jezebel pushed out an upstairs window to the pavement and then drove his chariot over her. Second Kings 9:33 spares no details: "Some of her blood spattered the wall and the horses as they trampled her underfoot."

Do you wonder if Joab ever thought of dying? Did Jezebel ever think about it? What about King Zechariah, who ruled Israel from his capital in Samaria? During the six months he held power, did he ever awaken in the night, his breath caught in his throat, imagining he could hear Death's tread across his shadow?

Did he, like Lincoln, have a premonition of death? When Shallum emerged from the crowd and rushed him, did he have a moment of horror before he felt the death blow? Was there time for any thought of God, or of his evil life, or of eternity? (2 Kings 15:8-10).

Contrast Zechariah's death with the mob action that took the life of Stephen. Stephen thought of God in his dying moments. He looked into Heaven and saw Jesus waiting. Dragged outside the city and stoned to death, he hardly noticed the rocks tearing and crushing his life away as he prayed, "Lord Jesus, receive my spirit" (Acts 7:54-60).

Like other histories, the Old Testament sometimes seems to run red with blood and death. We shudder as we read of parents sacrificing their children in fiery offerings to a heathen god (2 Kings 17:17), of soldiers butchering pregnant women (2 Kings 15:16), of Babylonians killing Zedekiah's sons as their father watched helplessly (2 Kings 25:7). We are appalled by the record of king after king being assassinated: Joash (2 Kings 12:20), Shallum (2 Kings 15:14), Pekahiah (2 Kings 15:25). We are shocked by the thought of ten thousand prisoners being thrown from a cliff to the rocks below (2 Chronicles 25:12).

Not everyone in the Bible died violently. Jacob died in bed (Genesis 49:33). So did Ahaziah, but not of old age (2 Kings 1:2, 16, 17). He was hurt in a fall through the lattice of his upstairs room, and his injuries proved fatal.

Many died in advanced age: Abraham's wife, Sarah, lived to be 127, Isaac to be 180, Joshua to be 110 (Genesis 23:1; 35:28; Joshua

24:29). Methuselah wins the trophy. Genesis 5:27 reads, "Altogether, Methuselah lived 969 years, and then he died." Think of all the funeral directors he outlived!

Samson was probably in his forties when he pulled the temple of Dagon down upon himself and thousands of revelers (Judges 16:23-30). Absalom may have been a little younger than that when his mule pinned his head in the oak branches, allowing Joab to pierce his still-living heart with three javelins (2 Samuel 18:9-15). In 1 Kings 2:34 we read that Joab met the end he had meted out to many others.

Death can come in strange ways.

A twenty-five-year-old marine, Corporal Richard Drown, died "of apparent respiratory arrest" when he choked on a mouthful of glazed donuts. Corporal Drown was a contestant in a donut-eating match that followed the Newport Pig Cooking Contest in Newport, North Carolina.

Drown swallowed four donuts successfully. While trying to swallow two more, he crammed yet another three into his mouth.

He gagged on those, but when someone said he had ten seconds left he stuffed three more in his mouth, walked off the stage and collapsed, according to Greg Pehrsen, another marine who was there.

Efforts to clear his airway were unsuccessful, and the medical team could not revive him.[3]

One of the strangest deaths in the Bible is recorded in Judges 4. Sisera, commander of the Canaanite army, fled from a losing battle and sought refuge in the tent of a woman named Jael. She gave him a drink of milk and he fell asleep, exhausted. Seeing her opportunity, Jael took a tent peg and a mallet, crept up to where Sisera lay sleeping, and pounded the thing through the side of his head.

Abimelech died when a woman dropped a millstone from a tower roof and crushed his skull (Judges 9:53), no doubt saving herself and her neighbors from a holocaust like that which incinerated about a thousand men and women in nearby Shechem (Judges 9:49). Jephthah's daughter came to a tragic end because of her father's rash vow (Judges 11).

An Ohio businessman, losing money on his restaurant, hired an accomplice to burn it down. Neither man got a cent, however, for the fire blazed out suddenly in the old building, trapped the arson-

---

3. Cleveland *Plain Dealer,* Monday, April 4, 1983.

ist, and burned him to death. Instead of insurance money, the restaurateur collected a prison sentence.

That is somewhat like what Zimri did (1 Kings 16:8-19). Plotting against Elah, king of Israel, Zimri came to Tirzah, caught the king when he was too drunk to defend himself, and murdered him. But Zimri lasted only seven days. The army, led by Omri, laid siege to Tirzah, forcing Zimri's retreat to the royal citadel, where he set the place on fire and died in the blaze.

Judas, too, died by his own hand (Matthew 27:5). Wounded, King Saul took his own life (1 Samuel 31:4). Ahithophel, his counsel to Absalom refused, hanged himself (2 Samuel 17:23).

Suicide is the eleventh most frequent cause of death in the United States, accounting for twenty-five thousand deaths annually. Among teens, suicide is second only to automobile accidents.

Of the two million Americans who die every year, eighty percent die in hospitals or nursing homes. Many others die quietly at home. In Bible times, too, many died in bed. Death came peacefully, as a sigh or a tired breath.

"Rehoboam rested with his fathers and was buried with them in the City of David" (1 Kings 14:31).

"Abijah rested with his fathers and was buried in the City of David" (1 Kings 15:8).

"Baasha rested with his fathers and was buried in Tirzah" (1 Kings 16:6).

For Further Research

1. Which is worse: to commit suicide with a fork or with a gun? Here are ten ways people can hasten their own deaths. Rate them according to what you think is the worst, next worst, and so on.

- reckless driving
- smoking
- not wearing seat belts
- using narcotics
- alcohol abuse
- overeating
- refusing medicine
- excessive worry
- not getting enough rest
- lack of exercise.

2. Ask a friend to rate this list and compare your rating with his.

"Jehoshaphat rested with his fathers and was buried with them in the city of David his father" (1 Kings 22:50).

"Jehoahaz rested with his fathers and was buried in Samaria" (2 Kings 13:9).

Azariah, afflicted with leprosy, "rested with his fathers and was buried near them in the City of David" (2 Kings 15:7). "Near them"—not *with* them. Leprosy was a dreaded disease, and even in death separated its victims from others.

Asa died of disease, and reading between the lines we can put together a grim picture.

> In the thirty-ninth year of his reign Asa was afflicted with a disease in his feet. Though his disease was severe, even in his illness he did not seek help from the Lord, but only from the physicians. Then in the forty-first year of his reign Asa died and rested with his fathers. They buried him in the tomb that he had cut out for himself in the City of David. They laid him on a bier covered with spices and various blended perfumes, and they made a huge fire in his honor.
> —2 Chronicles 16:12-14

Anyone who has smelled the stench of a gangrenous foot knows why spices and perfumes were needed during the funeral procession of a king with crowds lining the way to his burial place.

Abraham was 175 when he "breathed his last and died at a good old age, an old man and full of years; and he was gathered to his people" (Genesis 25:8). Methuselah lived 969 years.

Others died young. Jairus' daughter was only twelve (Mark 5:42). The baby born to David and Bathsheba lived just a short time (2 Samuel 12:15-19). And Jesus was only thirty-three.

Could today's doctors have saved Rachel from her death in childbirth? (Genesis 35:17, 18). Probably they would provide a different

---

For Further Research

3. Here are five ways you can shorten someone else's life. Rate them as you did the ways of shortening one's own life, Marking the worst one 5, the next worst one 2, and so on.

- *while hunting, mistaking a person for your quarry*
- *striking someone in uncontrolled anger*
- *driving an automobile while intoxicated*
- *leaving a gate open so a child falls down stairs*
- *horseplay at the lake, resulting in drowning.*
- *leaving a bottle of poison in reach of a child.*

4. Ask a friend to look over this list and rate the items. Compare your rating with his.

15

treatment for Hezekiah. Instead of a poultice of figs laid on the site of his infection (Isaiah 38:21), they would give him antibiotics. With the poultice, however, God granted him fifteen more years in answer to his prayer (Isaiah 38:1-5). In the end, death came to them all, just as it will come to you and to me.

Achan's disobedience brought death not only to himself but to his entire family (Joshua 7:24, 25). Another family died with no such disobedience as a cause. A boy was driving a big Lincoln eastbound toward Morehead, Kentucky, when it skidded on ice and slid sideways under the bumper of a big truck. He was only scratched, but his mother's body was crammed under the dash. His aunt was thrown out and died on the highway, and it took nearly three hours to separate what remained of his father from the wreckage.

Goliath was felled by a well-aimed rock (1 Samuel 17:49, 50). One of the prophets was mauled to death by a lion (1 Kings 13:24). Others died by accident (1 Kings 3:19), murder (Genesis 4:8), capital punishment (Genesis 40:22), drowning (Exodus 14:26-30), plague (Numbers 14:37), earthquake and fire (Numbers 16:31-35), snakebite (Numbers 21:6)—and not even yet have we exhausted the various ways death stalked and claimed its victims.

Death, like the Babylonian army, "spared neither young man nor young woman, old man or aged" (2 Chronicles 36:17).

Death Can Be Personal

Let's come closer to home. Five thousand Americans die *every day*, most from heart and circulatory problems. Dr. Maurice Rawlings tells us that "diseases of hardened arteries will kill more of us than will all other diseases put together."[4] Remember that when you eat your next order of greasy french fries. Cancer comes next, with accidents third.

Poets paint pretty pictures of death; songwriters try to soften death's impact with gentle words and soothing melodies, but reality remains. Death is there. Death waits. Death is coming.

We understand why the Persian emperor Xerxes wept after he had reviewed his expeditionary force, because he realized that not a single one of his soldiers would still be alive a hundred years later.[5]

4. Maurice Rawlings, M.D., *Before Death Comes* (Nashville, Thomas Nelson Publishers, 1980), p. 30. Used by permission.

5. Arnold J. Toynbee and Arthur Koestler, *Life After Death* (New York: McGraw Hill Book Co., 1976), pp. 3, 4.

Nor would he. Xerxes died too.
So did Herodotus, the historian who told us about it.
So will you.
And so will I.
Some day this heart will stop beating, these lungs will cease their life-support function; the vital spark we call life will go, and these

---

... the death of a near acquaintance aroused, as usual, in all who heard of it the complacent feeling that, "it is he who is dead and not I."
—Leo Tolstoi, in "The Death of Ivan Ilych"

---

bodies will chill and stiffen, death invading the brain first, then advancing cell by cell through the tissues, and finally bone.

The fact of your own death is as much a part of your life as the book you're holding now, as the furniture in the room where you're sitting. Maybe it will be three years from now, or thirty, or tomorrow, but some day death will come and your body will no longer function.

"Why rub it in?" you say. You don't like to think about it? No one else does, either. And don't feel bad because you have that reluctance. No sane, healthy person wants to die. It is good to think about living.

If you keep thinking about death and dying, you'll become depressed, anxious. You can become numb to life and may be a candidate for the place where they put padding on the walls and won't let you have anything sharp.

But do let's think about it a couple of minutes.

Suppose you were told you had only a year to live. Is there anything you'd want to do in the time left to you? Are there any changes you'd make in the way you are living now?

To be practical:

• Do you have a will? you don't have to be ninety-seven to write a will, you know.

• Does anyone else know where you keep your car keys? your bankbook?

• Is there a "Thank you" that you need to say to someone?

• Do you need to ask someone's forgiveness?

• Do you need to forgive someone?

- How about spending more time with your family, or taking your wife out for a romantic evening?
- Do you have a library book that is overdue?
- Is there a goal you've put off and put off, just waiting for the right time to go into action?

Suppose you did have one year to live. If there's something you would want to do in that year, better get cracking. He may not come in the next twelve months, but old Death is on his way, and maybe you won't be notified in advance when he comes.

When it comes down to it, though, it isn't death that's important. It is life.

You can become so afraid of death that you'll be afraid to live. Afraid to ride in a car because you might have an accident. Afraid to eat a hamburger because of the cholesterol. Afraid to breathe because your lungs might be polluted.

Go ahead and live. Accept the risks. You won't be here forever, so put as much into each day as you can. Ask, "Is what I'm doing now worth giving up part of my life to do it?"

Afraid of death? Then better get in touch with the only person who can really do something about it. He lived here too, and saw death firsthand. He knows what it does to people, to homes, to families. Standing by a friend's grave, He wept.

But that wasn't all He did.

He brought back that friend, back to life again! He brought back two others too. And after they had whipped and tortured Him and finally buried Him and sealed His tomb, He came back from the grave. Today He guarantees life after death to anyone who will accept His gift.

Think It Over

Fill in the blanks. How does it feel to write your own obituary-eulogy?

_____ died today at the age
(Write in your full name)

of _____. A native of
(age you think you're likely to die)

_____, _____ died
(your birthplace)   (he/she)

of _____.
(the way you think you may die)

He/she is most remembered for _____

_____.
(accomplishments you want to achieve in your life)

He/she is survived by _____.
(family members who may outlive you)

The funeral was conducted by _____, and the
(minister's name)

burial will be at _____.
(cemetery)

Where Did Death Come From?

Standing at Evelyn's bedside, one has to ask, "Why?" Her wasted body twisted so that her distended abdomen can lie almost like a separate thing beside her, yellowish eyes and sallow skin indicating that the disease has progressed to her liver: "Why?"

One wrist punctured by the I.V., her husband gently stroking the other and the NO CODE bracelet she has requested for this, which she knows will be her last hospital stay: "Why?"

Daughters Linda and Darla, mute in their grief, look at their mother and then at the visitor, asking, "Why?"

Why such pain, such suffering?

Why is Evelyn dying?

It's because of something that happened a long time before she was even born. She lived in a cancer-ridden world.

And how did the world get that way?

Genesis 3 tells us.

We've hardly finished reading of creation when we come to this record of disaster. At first it seems almost too simple. Can this brief explanation account for the blood and tears and death enshrouding the world?

You know what a determined terrorist can do to an airport or public building or embassy. That's a picnic compared to what happened here.

An Alien Comes on a Mission of Destruction

When the devil wants to do a dirty job, he puts on clean clothes. Before him lies God's creation: blue skies, clear air, open fields, pure water. Life everywhere! There go man and woman: intelligent, lovely, innocent.

How to gain entrance? If he can only find an opening! Disguised as a serpent, he comes to Eve, waiting until she is alone and most

---

Where there is no cure, all he has to do is infect one person.

---

vulnerable. Is she hungry, too? Now he tosses a question: "Did God really say you can't eat from every tree here?"

Subtly the question suggests just what Satan often suggests to us: "Is God trying to tell you what you can and can't do? What a shame He won't let you have any fun! Look, Eve, you ought to make your own decisions. You're your own person. Why should anyone boss you around?"

Rather than permitting Eve to see all the things she *can* do, Satan focuses her attention upon the one thing she cannot. The devil does the same with us.

"I know you're married, but look at that girl. Wouldn't you like to have her?"

"Yes, I know you have a lot of things, but here's something you don't have and you can rip it off easily."

"So you have your day all planned. Well, here's one item you ought to try. So it's forbidden? Who cares? Go ahead. Who's going to stop you?"

Eve is fascinated by all this. No one ever said sin is not appealing. It's exciting to listen to the serpent; exciting to think about something she has never thought about before, especially since that something is forbidden. "I wonder what 'evil' is?"

Haven't you experienced the same thing?

I remember, when I was in grade school, there was a hangout on the main street of our little town where older boys gathered. I knew they were not the kind my parents wanted me to be with, yet I remember how I used to like to walk past—better still, walk through—that crowd of roughnecks lounging on the sidewalk. I noticed their jackets and boots, and their coarse talk. I can almost see them now.

I was afraid of them. The danger itself was part of my excitement. Don't try to excuse Eve by saying she doesn't realize what she is doing. She knows she is getting closer and closer to forbidden territory, and the risk itself is part of the attraction.

Eve tells the serpent what God said—though perhaps she doesn't get it exactly right. It is not recorded that God said anything about *touching* the tree (Genesis 2:17). Did Adam add that when he told Eve about the commandment? Was it Eve's own addition? Or is it possible that God said more than is recorded in Genesis 2:17? In any case, Eve knows the tree is forbidden, and she says so.

Aha! She's talking to him. That's promising, from Satan's point of view. He presses his attack, trying to make it sound as if he's on her side.

"You won't die," Satan tells her. "God is not telling you everything. There are things He doesn't want you to know."

That must be an effective approach. Satan still uses it today: "Go ahead. How else will you find out what it's like?"

Now they are close to the tree. From here it looks even better.

It's not difficult to read Eve's thoughts: "Ummm. Doesn't that look good? Wonder what it would taste like. One time surely won't hurt. What's one little taste?"

> Commenting upon the widespread belief among the ancients that the world was originally perfect but fell into evil, the philosopher Immanuel Kant (1724-1804) offers his view:
>
> > More modern, though far less prevalent, is the contrasted optimistic belief, which indeed has gained a following solely among philosophers and, of late, especially among those interested in education—the belief that the world steadily (though almost imperceptibly) forges in the other direction, to wit, from bad to better; at least that the predisposition to such a movement is discoverable in human nature. If this belief, however, is meant to apply to *moral* goodness and badness (not simply to the process of civilization), it has certainly not been deduced from experience; the history of all times cries too loudly against it.[1]

1. Immanuel Kant, *Religion Within the Limits of Reason Alone* (New York, Harper and Row, 1960), p. 15.

Here is a new experience and it must be a stupid rule that would keep it from her. Who cares about rules, anyway?

What is it about evil that is so appealing, almost enchanting? So she takes the fruit. It doesn't hurt her when she touches it; a taste won't hurt her either, she thinks. If she doesn't like it she can spit it out.

So she goes ahead. But that is only a start. Not content to have broken God's law herself, she gives the fruit to Adam and he too eats it:

Result: Infection

Before we've tried something, the devil says, "Just one time. That won't hurt." After that one time, he says, "Don't quit now. You've already done it once; what's one more time?"

Then he says, "And get somebody else to do it with you." That has always been his pattern. First, he fell himself. Now he has corrupted Eve. And through her, Adam. Through them, the world.

From now on, the world will always be a mixture. The enemy has sown weeds in God's garden, and the bad is growing along with the good (Matthew 13:24-26).

You'll have a Metropolitan Art Gallery and the South Bronx in the same city; in the same hospital a newborn unit upstairs and a morgue down by the alley.

Sorrow has infected our joy, mixed tears into our laughter. In every good there is bad. The automobile, glad invention for

---

Fear. Fear. Fear.
The great harmony was lost. Chaos was loose.
                    —Harold Myra[2]

---

freedom and distance and speed, has maimed and butchered more Americans than all our wars put together.

In the same university we study food production and criminal law. We who were first to harness atoms were also first to drop them on civilians.

Does Eve know what she has done? Does Adam? The ground, which before meant such abundance, now brings forth thorns.

---

2. From *The Choice*, by Harold Myra. Published by Tyndale House Publishers, Inc., © 1980, p. 59. Used by permission.

Sweat if you want to eat, Adam! Eve, your femininity and charm, such joy before, will mean pain hereafter. Nor will it end with the birth. Eve, Eve! How you will weep when your Cain kills your Abel! Do you know what you've done, Eve?

Blame them? When we treat sin so lightly? Like a cold, we think, or spiritual sniffles, forgetting that sin is infinitely worse. Sin is deadly.

A malignancy in the body grows faster than normal, will invade other tissues, and can spread. According to the medical texts, a malignancy's most devastating property "is related to the ability of proliferating cancer cells to break away from the parent tumor (the so-called *primary* tumor) and enter the circulation to float elsewhere. When such embolic cancer cells lodge, they are able to extravasate, continue their proliferation, and form a *secondary* focus of tumor."[3]

In plain talk, the worst thing about cancer is that it spreads!

Evelyn's started in her abdomen. She had a colostomy, but that did not remove all the malignancy. Detected in her lymphoid system, it spread on into her lungs and into her brain.

Cancer cells don't act the way cells are supposed to. They do not obey the rules. They go out of control, taking new territory and turning normal cells into cancerous ones. Uncontrolled, they never stop until they have destroyed their host.

For Further Research

Check into these other references to the devil.

Matthew 4:1. *Devil* means slanderer.
Matthew 12:24, 27. *Beelzebub* means lord of filth.
Matthew 13:19. The evil one.
John 8:44. Murderer, liar, father of lies.
Acts 5:3. *Satan* means adversary.
2 Corinthians 4:4. The god of this age.
Ephesians 2:2. Ruler of the kingdom of the air.
1 Thessalonians 3:5. Tempter.
1 Peter 5:8. Enemy.
Revelation 9:11. *Abaddon* and *Apollyon* both mean destroyer.
Revelation 12:9. Great dragon, ancient serpent.

---

3. Sylvia Anderson Price and Lorraine McCarty Wilson, *Patho-Physiology, Clinical Concepts of Disease Processes* (New York, McGraw Hill Book Company, 1978), p. 93. Used by permission.

Sin does exactly the same. It spreads. It involves everyone it can infect. And in the end, it destroys.

Was God being vindictive when He told Adam and Eve what would happen because they had sinned?

No. He was stating simple truth.

Result: Defeat

You know how you feel when you've done wrong. You feel terrible. That sick feeling of guilt, that dread of being found out—that's what Adam and Eve felt. They wanted to hide. Don't we all? But no one really hides from God.

Sin wipes away our peace of mind, robs us of our joy and self-respect, leaves us depressed, hating ourselves, and with such a hopeless feeling.

Sin leads us away from what is pure and honorable and good. We're changed by it. "It is but one step, but it is like the step over a precipice or down the shaft of a mine; it cannot be taken back, it commits to an altogether different state of things."[4]

It's the feeling we've been beaten. It is knowing there was a contest between right and wrong, and we lost.

Paul describes it well: "I do not understand what I do. For what I want to do I do not do, but what I hate I do" (Romans 7:15).

I've felt that way. Haven't you? Maybe that is the way Eve feels,

For Further Research

Paul's comment in 1 Timothy 3:6 suggests that pride was Satan's downfall.

Some scholars think Isaiah's taunt against the king of Babylon is also a description of Satan's fall from Heaven, especially Isaiah 14:12-15.

Jesus came to destroy the work of the devil (1 John 3:8).

Through His death and resurrection, Jesus will destroy him who has the power of death, the devil (Hebrews 2:14).

Revelation 20 describes Satan's final end in the lake of fire.

Revelation 21 describes a home untouched by Satan.

---

4. W. Robertson Nicoll, ed., *The Expositor's Bible* (New York, A.C. Armstrong and Son, 1903), p. 23.

and Adam, too. Suddenly aware of what they have done, they try to cover their guilt. When God comes to them as He has often come before, they cannot face Him. They are ashamed. They are afraid. In terror they scurry out of sight among the trees, cowering before the voice they have welcomed before.

What is the difference? Does God call out, warning them, "You'd better run! I'm coming after you?"

No, it isn't like that. God comes seeking fellowship. He comes, as He often has come, to enjoy their friendship. But this time they don't want to see Him. Always before they have longed for these moments, but now they try to hide.

They know they are defeated. They are ashamed. Satan has shown them up. Satan has won; they have lost. Neither they nor the garden nor the world will ever be the same.

We are not the same, either. Because of them, the world became infected.

Was it entirely their fault? After all, they didn't put the tree there. They didn't make the rules.

Suppose there had never been a choice. Would that have been any better? At least they would never have fallen. Had there been no choice, there would have been no failure, no defeat.

But then what?

God used His infinite wisdom and power to make planet Earth and the plants and animals for these special beings He was making—beings who would have the power to think and feel and decide. If He then made them with no power to choose, that would mean that He somehow decided not to take the risk. That would mean a vast difference in the way God would make Adam and Eve.

Rather than let them fall, He would make them so they couldn't. He would give them everything else, but withhold *choice*. They would serve Him because there wasn't anything else they could do. The decision would be already made; God would have made it.

But look what this would have done. Without *choice* they would have nothing. They would only be furniture, decoration, part of the landscape. And they would never find out about love or obedience or devotion. They would have been puppets, not persons.

You can't love someone if you don't have choice. To love, you have to *choose*.

If you can choose to love, you can choose not to love. And if you can choose to obey, you can also choose to disobey. The possibility has to be there.

26

That precious gift of freedom offered Satan his opportunity, and he—the liar—deceived them into falling into sin. The damage was done.

When Neil Armstrong, Michael Collins, and "Buzz" Aldrin returned from the first landing on the moon, they emerged from *Columbia* wearing biological isolation garments and went immediately to a specially adapted vacation trailer known as the Mobile Quarantine Facility on the recovery ship USS *Hornet*. From there they went to Hawaii and then by plane to the Lunar Receiving Laboratory at Houston.

Why all the precautions? To be sure they were not bringing back organisms that could destroy life on earth.

Result: Death

The astronauts did not turn loose some new and deadly virus on earth, but Adam and Eve did; rather, Satan did when he infected them with sin. Before their sin, life everywhere. Afterward, death; everywhere death. Ruefully our grandfathers commented that only two things are sure; death and taxes.

Sin brings death. Adam's sin brought death not only to him but to the whole race. Sadly God tells Adam what he has done:

> Cursed is the ground because of you;
> through painful toil you will eat of it
> all the days of your life.
> It will produce thorns and thistles for you,
> and you will eat the plants of the field.
> By the sweat of your brow
> you will eat your food
> until you return to the ground,
> since from it you were taken;
> for dust you are
> and to dust you will return.
> —Genesis 3:17-19

God is the source of life. When Adam and Eve separate themselves from God, they separate themselves from life. Death is inevitable.

They have to leave the garden. They are not allowed to have the tree of life. They've separated themselves from all that. That's gone. That's past. They've lost it.

And they have lost it for us, too. They lost it for Evelyn. She slipped further and further into the coma. Nurses began to come every two hours to turn her over to prevent bedsores, because her limbs and body had become so emaciated that her bones almost protruded. Had she done some terrible thing that caused her to contract the disease? Not at all. She had committed sins, yes; but

---

... sin entered the world through one man,
and death through sin.
—Romans 5:12

---

she had already brought her sins to Jesus and let Him wash them away. She had died to her sins by being buried with Him in baptism (Romans 6:1-4). She was not suffering now because of any sin she had committed. But she had been born into a world where there was suffering and death.[5] As Paul wrote to the church at Corinth, "In Adam all die" (1 Corinthians 15:22).

You say, "It's not fair! Why did all this happen as a result of Adam's sin? Why should we die because of Adam?"

Who ever said Satan was fair? Ask the child battered to death if an innocent person ever dies because of someone else's sin. Two little girls on the way home from the store were run over and killed by a drinking driver; ask their mother if someone can die because of another person's sin. Ask the victim of a senseless murder.

Satan is anything but fair. Not for nothing does the Bible call him the "destroyer" (Revelation 9:11). He knew that all he had to do was find one person who would open the door. Once sin was turned loose in the world, death would follow.

When the Nazis came to the Russian village of Ustinovka, they destroyed everything. Most of the houses were in ruins, the thatched roofs blown away by bomb blasts, the townspeople driven away or dead. An old man and two little boys came back and lived by digging up potatoes from the deserted gardens.

The only other person in the village was an old blind woman who had lost her mind during the shelling. Barefoot, she wandered from house to house, kept alive because one of the boys shared his potatoes with her. She carried a few dirty rags, a pail, and a tattered

---

5. Evelyn died soon after this was written.

sheepskin, and as she stumbled through the ruined town she kept muttering the word *cherti*—the devils.[6]

Likewise in Eden the invader had come, and had brought death with him.

Think It Over

1. Satan came to the garden on a mission of destruction. Jesus came to earth on a different kind of mission. Check these passages and see what His mission was: Matthew 5:17; 20:28; Luke 4:43; 19:10; John 3:16, 17; 9:39; 10:10; 12:47; 18:37.

2. Christ cures sin's infection, as shown in Isaiah 53:4-6 and Romans 5:6-8.

3. Christ gives victory over defeat and shame. See such Scriptures as John 16:33; Romans 7:21-25; and 1 Corinthians 15:51-57.

4. Christ brings life where Satan has brought death. Look up John 11:25; 14:1-6; and Romans 5:12-21.

You may want to discuss these Scriptures with a friend and talk over how Jesus gives us back everything Satan took away from us.

6. Alexander Werth, *Russia at War* (New York, Avon Books, 1964), p. 199.

"Your daughter is dead. . . .
Why bother the teacher any more?"
                                 —Said to Jairus

This Conqueror Fought Death

You know their names. Each one a conqueror. Napoleon Bonaparte. Adolf Hitler. Julius Caesar. Genghis Khan. Alexander the Great. Men whose power swept everything before them.

Which one was the greatest?

Hitler's "Thousand Year Reich" lasted only twelve years, four months, and eight days; but that was long enough to turn Europe into a wasteland and bring millions to their graves. And Hitler? He shot himself rather than face capture.

Julius Caesar invaded Helvetia, then Gaul, bridged the Rhine, crossed the Marne, Meuse, Sambre, and Somme Rivers, conquered most of Europe, crossed the channel, and defeated the British.

Coming home, he met opposition from Pompey and halted his legions while the Roman Senate "investigated."

Seizing the moment, he crossed the Rubicon, a little stream marking the border of Rome proper, and marched on the capital. On August 9, 48 B.C., he met Pompey in battle, and by sundown was master of his world.

Born in a little room in Ajaccio, on the island of Corsica, August 5, 1769, Napoleon left home at nine to be educated in France as a soldier. By the age of twenty-four he was a brigadier general, and less than two years later was named Commander in Chief of the French Army in Italy.

Immediately he struck at the enemy, defeating both the Italian and the Austrian armies. Next came Egypt, and a crushing defeat to a Turkish army sent against him.

Frustrated by his inability to invade Britain, he conquered Prussia, then moved against Spain. Leaving others to continue the Spanish campaign, in the summer of 1812 Napoleon marched on Russia and by October was in Moscow.

Alexander left Macedonia with only thirty thousand foot soldiers and five thousand cavalry, invaded Asia Minor, destroyed the Persian Army under Darius III, marched around the eastern rim of the Mediterranean, down into Egypt, eastward again to Babylon, and all the way to India. In a decade Alexander the Great had conquered the world.

A tribal chieftain before he was twenty, Genghis Khan rose to power using Karakorum, "the City of the Black Sands," as his base. For thirty years he fought off rivals until by the age of fifty he had welded the tribes of Central Asia into one united force with him as sole leader.

Now he attacked China, forcing through the Great Wall to the capital. Next he swept down upon Samarkand, then came westward to the Middle East, through Russia, and across Central Europe.

The armies of China, the warriors of Islam, and the knights of Christendom all fled before his fierce Mongols. From the Pacific to Central Europe, embracing most of the then-known world and more than half its population—all was his.

Conquest in Galilee
Mark 5:21-24, 35-43

Reading the reports of Jesus' teaching and of His healing ministry, we're not surprised that people followed Him. Here, by the Sea of Galilee, a large crowd presses around Him, straining to hear, many standing on tiptoe for a better view.

Suddenly there is a hush, and the crowd parts to let a man through. Many recognize him at once. What can this well-dressed ruler of the synagogue want with the teacher from Nazareth?

Synagogues were places where devout Jews met to worship God and to study the Scriptures. The synagogue rulers were responsible for the building, had oversight of the worship, selected those who were to read the Scriptures, to pray, and to speak.

When Jesus began His Galilean ministry He often taught in the synagogue. When He returned to His hometown and went to the synagogues, it seemed at first that the people were going to listen; but as Jesus talked they became so angry they drove Him out and tried to kill Him (Luke 4:15-30).

As the months passed Jesus was no longer so welcome in the synagogues. More and more He used the out-of-doors, teaching on a hillside, or as He walked, or from a boat put out a short distance from the listening crowd along the beach.

The attitude of most synagogue rulers had turned to cautious skepticism or even open hostility. Jairus risked his reputation and perhaps his position by coming to Jesus.

But Jairus cared little about that. He was not thinking of his social standing; he could only recall the awful scene back home where his little girl lay deathly ill. There were no hospitals, no skilled doctors, no medicines to speak of; only an anxious mother bathing the girl's burning face and arms, trying to bring down the fever. Maybe Jesus could help.

Jairus fell at Jesus' feet and pleaded, "My little daughter is dying. Please come and put your hands on her so that she will be healed and live" (Mark 5:23).

Immediately Jesus started off with Jairus, and Jesus' disciples came along. They had not gone far when a woman in the crowd—she had been sick for a long time—stopped Jesus. By the time He had

---

When once our brief light sets, there is but one perpetual night through which we must sleep.
—Catullus, Roman poet

---

healed her, men came from Jairus' house with the word, "Your daughter is dead. Why bother the teacher any more?" To them, it was the end. Too late now for Jesus.

The messengers could hardly have come at a worse time. A thousand thoughts must have raced through Jairus' mind: "Why did He have to stop for that old woman? She's lived her life. If she had not interrupted him, my daughter might be. . . ."

Jesus ignored the messengers and turned to Jairus. "Don't be afraid; just believe." Keep your faith strong, Jairus. I am still here, and will come to your house and see your daughter.

Jesus took Peter, James, and John; and the little group left. Before they reached the house they could tell which one it was by the crowd and the noise. So that no one would die unmourned, the custom developed that mourners would come and share a family's grief. Matthew 9:23 even mentions flute players. Apparently they had been summoned quickly to add their doleful music to the wailing of the sorrowful friends.

Burial took place the same day a person died, so the mourners were probably neighbors. Out-of-town people could hardly have had time to get there.

Jesus went into the house and quieted the crowd. "Why all this?" He asked. "She is sleeping." Later on Jesus would use the word "sleep" in connection with another death (John 11:11, 14). He can wake the dead as easily as we wake a sleeper. But even the disciples didn't understand that when Jesus spoke of death as sleep, and of course the mourners didn't understand.

Instead of quickening hope, Jesus' statement met doubt and scorn. He ordered everyone out of the house immediately, except for the three disciples and girl's parents. Jesus had no intention of permitting this act of mercy to become a circus feat.

Quiet descended upon the little group as they gathered around the bed where the girl's body lay. The voice of the crowd outside faded into the background; the only sound in here was a mother's sobbing.

Jesus moved to the girl's bedside, reached out and took her hand, and spoke only two words: *"Talitha koum!"* [1]

Instantly the girl opened her eyes, stood, looked at her parents, at Jesus, at the three strangers, started walking around and talking. She was unharmed; she was well! Completely well!

None of those in that room had ever seen anything like this before. What had the father asked Jesus? Little did he realize how literally his request would be carried out: "Please come and put your hands on her so that she will be healed and live."

Everyone thought death had won. Jesus stepped onto the battlefield, took death's victim by the hand, and led her to life.

No other conqueror can match this. Not even Alexander the Great. Though he had conquered the world, death finally defeated him. He entered Babylon in the spring of 323 B.C. for what was to be his last time. Exhausted, suffering the effects of his wounds and excessive drinking, he developed a fever and died. Alexander was about thirty-three years old.

---

1. Aramaic for "Little girl, get up."

The Conqueror Comes to Nain
Luke 7:11-17

Jesus was in His second year of ministry, and people from all over Judea, from Jerusalem, and from the seacoast of Tyre and Sidon had come to hear Him and to be healed of their diseases (Luke 6:17-19).

Many went with Him to Capernaum, where He healed the servant of a Roman centurion (Luke 7:1-10), and out through the hills of Galilee. They came to Nain, a little village set on the northwest slope of the Hill of Moreh, not far from Nazareth. Coming up the road toward the village they met a funeral coming out of the city gate, going to the cemetery. The dead were buried apart from the living, and the body may have been destined for one of the rock-hewn sepulchres on the hillside.

It would be difficult to picture a more pathetic scene. Dressed in mourning clothes was the tiny figure of a woman, alone, supported by her grieving friends. There was no husband, for she had earlier accompanied his body to this same burial place. Then it was her son who had walked beside her, comforting her and offering strength. Now he was gone too. What would she do without him? How could she go on living?

The coffin was not like our steel or wood caskets, but was more like a stretcher, with the body lying on it, first washed and wrapped in a burial cloth. If the family could afford it, the body would be anointed with aromatic spices and ointments. There was no embalming as we think of it, and burial usually took place on the day of death.

Jesus saw the situation at once, and His heart went out to the grieving mother. "Don't cry," He said. We should never feel that He is unmoved by our tears.

Jesus knew the regulations that anyone who touched the dead became unclean (Numbers 19:11). Still He went up and touched the bier, so that those carrying it stopped.

They may have known Jesus, considering how close Nazareth was. They had certainly heard of Him. Whether or not the bearers expected what happened next would be difficult to say. They did not wait long.

"Young man, I say to you, get up!"

In our funeral practice, when family and friends pass by the body before the casket is closed, sometimes a mourner will say something to the departed, knowing the corpse cannot hear, and without expecting an answer. The words are not spoken for the benefit of the dead but for the speaker, as he or she expresses sorrow or regret or some other emotion.

Jesus' approach was entirely different. He spoke, but not to release feelings of grief. Nor was He making idle comment. He spoke *to* the dead person, expecting a response *from* the dead person.

If you've ever been seriously ill, you know how weak and helpless you feel afterward. Patients recuperating from such illness often need help to stand upon their feet that first time. This young man, terribly sick, sick enough that he died, sat up and started talking. He needed no help. He was ready to go home.

Luke said little about the sorrow, and now he says little about the joy. He leaves to our imagination the gasp of astonishment from the crowd; the shocked faces of the pallbearers (Did they almost drop the corpse suddenly come to life?); the mother's cry of joy; glad tears replacing tears of sadness.

Did the young man tell of the world from which he had returned, as so many have described "after death" experiences? If he did, Luke says nothing about it. Neither does the Bible record such information from others who were raised from the dead

Luke says only that "Jesus gave him back to his mother." She had thought he was gone forever. Jesus brought him back. No wonder "news about Jesus spread."

Jesus left the scene in triumph, in sharp contrast to Napoleon's disintegration in Russia. Yes, Napoleon did march on Russia June 24, 1812. Yes, he did reach Moscow by October. But the tattered rabble that entered Moscow bore slight resemblance to *the Grand Armee* that had crossed the Niemen.

Kutuzov, the Russian commander, had continuously retreated, drawing Napoleon deeper into enemy territory, farther from his supply lines. Disease and weariness and battles at Smolensk and Borodino took their toll. Expecting to find shelter, food, and an offer of peace in Moscow, Napoleon found a deserted city set on fire by its defenders. He had to turn back. Distance, lack of discipline, and the Russian winter did the rest.

Bring life to the dead? Oh no, not Napoleon. He did just the opposite. In his sixty battles he caused so many casualties that historians are hard put to count them. Estimates range from 450,000 to 1,750,000!

But in the end, death defeated him. Sick, exiled on lonely St. Helena in the South Atlantic, Napoleon breathed his last on May 5, 1821.

Victory in a Family Cemetery
John 11:1-44

The scene shifts from Galilee, where Jairus' daughter and the widow's son were raised, to Judea and the town of Bethany, not quite two miles from Jerusalem. Other things have changed, too. Crowds are still with Jesus, but the authorities in Jerusalem have become so hostile that Jesus has withdrawn to the far side of the Jordan (John 10:40-42).

He is there when a message comes from two sisters at Bethany: "Lord, the one you love is sick." Mary and Martha know that is all they need to say. From that brief word Jesus will know that Lazarus is seriously ill, and Jesus will come immediately. This must have been their hope, though they knew the danger in Jerusalem.

But no, Jesus delays, saying that Lazarus' sickness will not end in death, but that God will work through this illness to bring glory to God's Son.

By hurrying to Bethany, Jesus might reach the house in time to heal Lazarus, or to bring him back after only minutes of death, as in the case of Jairus' daughter, or after a few hours, as with the widow's son. The sisters would appreciate that, of course.

By not going at once, Jesus will do more than a miracle of healing, and show more than that He is a great prophet (see Luke 7:16). He will show that He is Lord of Life and Conqueror of Death. Earlier He said,

I tell you the truth, a time is coming and has now come when the dead will hear the voice of the Son of God and those who hear will live.
—John 5:25

For Further Research

Compare Jesus' miracles with some others.

Jesus heals leprosy with a touch (Matthew 8:3) or simply through His will (Luke 17:11-14). Contrast Moses' pleading in Numbers 12:13-15.

With some ceremony, Elijah and Elisha call on the Lord to raise the dead (1 Kings 17:19-23; 2 Kings 4:29-36). Jesus simply says, "Get up" or "Come out" (Mark 5:41; Luke 7:14; John 11:43).

Peter says, "Get up," but only after fervent prayer. The result is faith in Jesus, not Peter (Acts 9:40-42).

What does all this suggest about the power of Jesus?

He said it. Now He will demonstrate it. He says, "This sickness will not end in death." Jesus already has decided what He will do when He reaches Bethany.

John inserts the statement that Jesus loved Martha, Mary, and Lazarus, perhaps because he thinks it may look as if Jesus were neglecting their request. Sometimes God, because of His love and not in spite of it, does not give what we ask but waits to give us something far better. Jesus will do that here.

He is going to show what He can do in a situation that is utterly hopeless, when people are utterly helpless and feel that God has not answered their need. Jesus will show that even in the most terrible and permanent situation—death—He is still able to exercise absolute control.

Jesus' disciples are alarmed when He suggests going back to Judea. They remember the recent attempt on His life (John 10:31), and think He will be in danger in Judea. Events are to prove them right (John 18, 19).

Jesus answers them, but not directly, saying that so long as it is daylight, a man can see to do what he needs to do. Then He answers directly, telling them that He is going to Bethany to raise Lazarus. Has a second messenger brought word of Lazarus' death? No. Jesus *knows.*

But the disciples miss what Jesus is saying. A messenger has come saying Lazarus is ill. They have seen that. They also have noticed that Jesus does not start immediately to Bethany. Maybe Lazarus isn't as sick as his sisters think. When Jesus speaks of Lazarus' sleeping, they think his fever has broken and the crisis is past. But Jesus soon corrects that thought.

"Lazarus is dead." They cannot mistake those words. Then Jesus tells the disciples He is glad that He was not there when Lazarus died, because what He will do will strengthen their faith.

When they reach Bethany, Lazarus has been buried four days.

The family seems to be wealthy. Later, Mary will give an offering worth a year's wages (John 12:5), and earlier their home accommodated Jesus and His disciples for an elaborate meal (Luke 10:38-42). Now the house is filled with those who have come to express sympathy with the sisters in their loss.

Martha hears of Jesus' arrival first. Her greeting shows what she and her sister have so often said to each other over the past four days: "If Jesus had just been here...." Did they think He had let them down?

Her next statement shows her high regard for Him: "Even now God will give you whatever you ask." It is as if she were saying, "You can pray and God will hear Your prayer and raise my brother." But does she fully realize that He himself is divine?

Jesus answers in a manner that forces Martha to probe deeper into her thinking. Her reply shows belief in a resurrection and future life. Now Jesus brings the focus away from the distant future to the immediate present. See John 11:25, 26.

He is saying to her, "The victory over death, Martha, is in me. Life is in me. If you trust in me, then you don't have to worry about death anymore." Jesus treats death as a minor incident when it concerns the believer.

Does Martha believe this? She did not hear Peter make his great confession of faith (Matthew 16:16), but on her own Martha has formed a firm and settled conviction. Look at John 11:27.

For centuries her people have longed for the Messiah, and one of the Messiah's powers is to raise the dead. She answers, "I know You are the Messiah we've hoped and prayed for." Then she calls Mary.

Mary's first words echo Martha's opening statement to Jesus: "If You had been here."

Jesus sees her grief, and Martha's, and the grief of their friends. He is deeply affected by their sorrow. Those two words, "Jesus wept," forever tell us that God cares about our sorrows and sympathizes with our needs.

They take Jesus to a tomb cut out of rock, with a stone door laid across the entrance. Martha, so strong before, so convinced before

---

Deep into that darkness peering, long I stood there wondering, fearing,
Doubting, dreaming dreams no mortals ever dared to dream before.

—from Poe's "The Raven"

(John 11:27), now begins to waver. She is not thinking of Jesus' power; she is thinking of what four days in that hot climate would do to her brother's body.

After the stone has been moved to one side, Jesus offers a simple prayer so those witnessing this will know that His power comes from His oneness with the Father.

Jesus can see into the next world as plainly as we see in this. He is not shouting into the darkness. He sees Lazarus and calls to him.

In that other world Lazarus hears and responds. Four days ago Lazarus left that body that is already beginning to decompose, but now he returns. What has been wrapped in burial garb and consigned to the ground begins to live and move and breathe again.

No one talks about "a great prophet" or some other lesser title. Look at the reaction to this miracle:

> Therefore many of the Jews who had come to visit Mary, and had seen what Jesus did, put their faith in him.
>
> —John 11:45

Genghis Khan fought all-out war. Those who resisted him, he killed to the last man. In one city alone, five hundred thousand civilians were slaughtered. But this military genius, this agent of terror and death, died in a campaign in 1227 at the age of sixty-six. He had conquered his world, but he could not conquer death.

Think It Over

1. Did Lazarus come back as a person? As a disembodied spirit? As something else? What does this tell you about the resurrection?

2. When Lazarus came back, could his sisters recognize him? Did either say, "This isn't our brother?" See John 12:2. What about the neighbors? Did they say, "That isn't Lazarus?" Look at John 12:9. Could Jesus' enemies argue that Jesus had not really brought Lazarus back from the dead? See John 12:10, 11. Does this say anything to you about the resurrection?

3. In the place where he was, was Lazarus conscious or unconscious? Could he hear? Could he know anything? Could he make any response? Does this seem to indicate anything about the dead? What do you think it may show?

4. In these three resurrections, did any of the three persons merge with "the vast spiritual reality in back of the universe" when they died? Or did they maintain their individuality? How do you know? Does this say anything to you about what will come after death?

5. What does Jesus show us in the raising of these three in regard to His own control over death and life?

*Sometimes they dissolve, the way this man is dissolving,
with everything running out of 'em—life, hope, soul, consciousness.
There's no doubt about this man. He's dying.*
                    —*The London print seller, in* Northwest Passage[1]

What Is It Like to Die?

"DEAD MAN FELT GOOD" read the headline in our Canton *Repository* for Tuesday, August 8, 1983.

"I know this sounds weird," said John Loughry, 29, after he had been hit by lightning, "but I could see myself in the ambulance and them giving me electric shocks to start my heart. I thought, 'What are they doing? Why don't they leave me dead? I feel good.'"

Loughry knows he is lucky to be alive, but he says his brush with death was a fascinating experience. For a quite different perspective, come to the death room of the Texas prison where Charlie Brooks, convicted of killing David Gregory, is to be the first person in the United States to be executed by injection.

Dick J. Reavis, writing in the *Texas Monthly*, describes what it was like to walk down the hall and enter the death room where Brooks was already strapped to the gurney that would become his death-bed.

> We filed in, and those of us who were nearest the gurney placed our hands on the black metal railing that stood between us and Charlie Brooks. All of us, I'm sure, saw him

1. Kenneth Roberts, *Northwest Passage* (Garden City, Doubleday and Company, Inc., 1936, 37), pp. 366, 367. Used by permission.

before we turned toward the railing. Most of us had already been shocked by the look on his face.... I couldn't take my eyes off Charlie. The muscles in his face were taut, his cheeks nearly flattened, like those of a motorcyclist speeding into a strong, cold wind. He was scared.[2]

Moments later the signal was given and the IV carried the lethal sodium thiopental, pancurinium bromide, and potassium chloride into his bloodstream.

Brooks' head turned slowly back and forth as if he were saying "No," then a sound like a sigh came from his lips; for a few seconds his body lay flat and still, then he struggled for breath, his fingers trembling with the exertion, and he was still. Charlie Brooks was dead.

Death Means Different Things
to Different People

For Saul, Israel's first king, death meant the sad and sorry end to a disappointing life. Impressive as a young man, tall and strong, Saul began his rule with great promise. In the opening days of his reign the Ammonites invaded Israel, and in a brilliant campaign Saul united his people and defeated the enemy with a daring nighttime raid (1 Samuel 11:1-11).

Alas, his first victory was his greatest, and he soon distinguished himself for his poor judgment. He failed as a leader, failed as a father, failed in his dealings with David, failed as a spiritual figure.

Wounded, his troops retreating, Saul could not even induce his armor-bearer to dispatch him, but had to fall on his sword himself, thus ending his tragic life (1 Samuel 31:3, 4).

For melodrama, consider the fate of George, Duke of Clarence, and brother of Edward IV, King of England. Clarence was only twenty-eight years old and a born scoundrel. His conceit and rashness led him into repeated schemes against his brother the king. The government was patient with him, but not forever. Parliament finally sentenced him to death.

The sentence was carried out February 17 or 18, 1478, in the Tower of London, creating one of those mysteries that enliven dull history textbooks. According to persistent rumor—never denied by

---

2. Dick J. Reavis, "Charlie Brooks' Last Words." Reprinted with permission from the February issue of *Texas Monthly*. Copyright 1983 by *Texas Monthly*.

any of those involved—Clarence was drowned at his own request in a large cask of malmsey, a sweet and expensive wine.[3]

Sometimes death cuts off a distinguished career, as in the case of John F. Kennedy. Revisionists have debated whether he would have attained such an honored place in the nation's memory if he had not been struck down so dramatically, but all can agree that Kennedy was at the peak of his career when he was shot.

The case of Hezekiah offers a parallel, though without the presence of a Lee Harvey Oswald. According to the record, Hezekiah "was successful in whatever he undertook" (2 Kings 18:7). He instituted needed reforms, repulsed Assyria, defeated the Philistines, and during the ensuing peace was able to provide a public-works program that brought among other things a water supply to his capital city.

At the height of his achievements he developed an infection and was told he could not live. Hezekiah turned his face to the wall, praying and weeping, asking God to spare him. The Lord heard Hezekiah's prayer and extended his life by fifteen years (2 Kings 20:1-6).

No such warning came to Lincoln. The assassin's bullet cut him down in mid-career. At least Lincoln saw the Union saved. Dr. Martin Luther King, also cut down in the midst of an influential life, did not live to see his dream realized.

To Everyone, Death Is Inevitable

We never quite come to terms with death. No matter how strong our faith, deep within each of us lies an unspoken uneasiness about death. Our own personal death is such a terrible thought that we can hardly think about it.

We hear statements such as "All men are mortal. Socrates is a man. Therefore, Socrates is mortal." This seems perfectly correct when it concerns Socrates, but somehow quite different when applied to oneself.

We all have a subconscious list of those we feel will die before we do.

Does a tree know that it will die? Ludicrous, you say. Does an earthworm, lifted out of the bait can, know that its time has come? Still ludicrous.

3. Thomas B. Costain, *The Last Plantagenets* (New York, Popular Library, Doubleday and Company, 1962), pp. 335-41.

But what about a dog? Does a dog know that it will die? Haven't you heard about an old dog going off by itself to die? Or is this just a story, a fable, an old wives' tale?

Does a steer, hauled from the feedlot to the slaughterhouse, know what it means when he sees the man with the mallet?

Does any other creature in the entire universe know that the day will come when it will lie still and cold in death? Know this nearly all of its life?

In the climax of creation, when the Lord God bent over the earth and swept up a handful of dust and shaped the first man and then breathed life into his nostrils, we began to live. In that dark hour when the man and his partner rebelled against their Maker and opened the door to sin, we began to die. And we have not stopped dying since.

Nurse Sarah tells about one of her patients:

The patient was a thirty-nine-year-old male who came to our floor after open-heart surgery. As I am thirty-nine myself, it was very difficult for me to see this man in trouble.

When I walked into his room his face was the color of a piece of paper. He didn't have any blood pressure, and I immediately got the doctor and told him, "This man doesn't belong on my floor."

The patient was then transferred to intensive care, and from there taken to surgery, where they opened his chest and drained about a pint of fluid from the infection that had developed. He was now a very sick man.

He came through the second surgery, however, and went home, coming into the hospital for tests and blood work. One day he stopped by my station and said he was having some trouble. His incision had not healed, and he had an area about an inch and one-half long that was still open and draining. That same week he was readmitted.

"I don't know what's wrong," he told me when I went to his room to see him. "I haven't worked in two years. We're out of money. My wife and I are quarreling and I don't know what to do."

"Right now let's concentrate on getting better," I told him.

He was lethargic, had fever, didn't want to eat. That night they put him on telemetry to keep track of his heartbeat in case he ran into more trouble.

I had just come on duty next morning when we had an emergency page from his room. I ran down the hall and met the night nurse coming for the crash cart. Blood was spurting from his incision. No time to lose!

During the next hour we used five cartons of four by fours—large surgical pads—to try to stop the bleeding. He had four IV lines in him giving him blood.

He was awake during all this and that made it harder for us because we had to watch everything we were saying. He was very frightened and kept saying, "Am I dying?" We kept telling him, "We are doing everything we can. Hang on."

I called the man's home and reached his fourteen-year-old son and told him we had to take his father to surgery again.

The son said, "Is my father dying? I have been the man for two years at my house. Tell me."

So I told him. "Yes, I think your dad is dying. It will take a miracle to save him."

As we were taking him to surgery, the man grabbed my hand. "Sarah, tell my wife I love her, because we fought last night."

He died just when they got him on the operating table. His family sent us a card thanking us for what we did and because we cared.

Some have sought means of avoiding death. Juan Ponce de Leon discovered Florida, but we don't remember him for that. We've all heard about his supposed search for the fountain of youth. Oh yes, he died in 1521.

King Josiah tried another approach. No fountain of youth for him; he used a disguise. Warned not to go into battle, Josiah went anyway. The enemy could not tell him from any of his men, but still an arrow found him. Josiah should have remembered Ahab. The same thing happened to him. (See 2 Chronicles 35:20-24 and 1 Kings 22:29-37.)

Will There Be Pain?

We shudder when we read Elijah's warning to King Jehoram, and shudder even more reading of its fulfillment. Jehoram's godless ways brought him to ruin, and Elijah's prediction came terribly true.

> After all this, the Lord afflicted Jehoram with an incurable disease of the bowels. In the course of time, at the end of the second year, his bowels came out because of the disease, and he died in great pain.
>
> —2 Chronicles 21:18, 19

44

King Herod, grandson of the Herod who ordered the death of the male children at Jesus' birth, also died horribly. He was "now at the zenith of his power, and was living in the utmost magnificence"[4] when he ascended his throne during a festival in honor of Claudius Caesar, arrayed in a robe of woven silver. His audience shouted approval: "This is the voice of a god, not of a man!" Herod loved it.

Suddenly Herod was seized with great pain as "an angel of the Lord struck him down, and he was eaten by worms and died" (Acts 12:22, 23). The historian Josephus says that Herod lingered in great torture for five days before he died.

Little Danny felt no pain when he died. His heart had not developed properly, and his parents knew he could not live long.

He did not gain as he should have, and every cold or earache was cause for concern. One bout was worse then the others, and the doctor put Danny in the hospital.

For Further Research

Can you think of other euphemisms we use to keep from saying "He died"? Here are several: "He cashed in his chips," "He bought the farm," "He croaked," "He passed away."

The Bible doesn't always use the same term, either. Look up these verses and see who it was who died and how the death is described.

Genesis 25:8
Genesis 49:33
2 Chronicles 16:13
2 Chronicles 21:20
Job 3:17
Daniel 12:2
Mark 5:39
John 19:30
Acts 5:5, 10
Acts 13:36
1 Thessalonians 4:13.

He developed a high fever and, despite the efforts of the medical team, began to fail. Gradually his breathing became more and more shallow and his pulse weaker, though more rapid. Toward the last his heart slowed and stopped.

The only pain he felt was the slight prick from the injections given in the attempt to prolong his life.

My friend Roy felt no pain, either. After his last heart attack, we all knew he could not live, and the family called me about ten o'clock on Saturday night. Roy was awake when I walked into his room, and talked with me and with his wife and grown daughter who were at his bedside.

---

4. J. W. McGarvey, *Acts of Apostles* (Cincinnati, Standard Publishing Company), pp. 232, 241.

As the hours passed we could see that he was getting weaker. Roy knew, and we knew, that he would not live through the night. I reached into my pocket for my Testament and Psalms, and began reading Psalm 23.

The only sounds in the room were the whisper of the oxygen, the sound of my voice, and the quiet sobs of his family.

Roy was with us as I began the familiar words. When I had finished, I looked up and Roy was gone.

The next day both his wife and daughter and two of Roy's grandchildren were in church, and their voices were among the strongest in singing the hymns of the faith. Roy was safe beyond the valley of the shadow of death.

Martha, a nurse, remembers one of her patients:

The patient was a six-year-old female victim of an auto-pedestrian accident. She was brought in on Friday afternoon to the ICU with severe trauma to the brain stem resulting in respiratory and heart failure.

She was totally unresponsive. She was deeply unconscious. There were no brain waves on the EEG. There was no evidence of feeling, no evidence of pain or anything.

The thing that was so difficult was to see the parents' feelings and know there was little we could do. We could only provide supportive care to the child, and do what we could for them as well, trying to answer their questions truthfully and permit them to vent their feelings. We cried with them. Sometimes I think that may be the best you can do for people in a situation like this.

The little girl died that Saturday afternoon.

Will there be pain? Perhaps. Perhaps not. But it seems, according to those who have stood closest to death, that in far more times than not there is no pain at the moment of death.

Dr. Maurice Rawlings writes,

The experience seems uniform: Actual death has no sting, no pain. The condition leading to death—the crushing auto accident, for instance—may be quite painful, but death itself is like a simple faint, a missed heartbeat, like going to sleep.[5]

---

5. Maurice Rawlings, M.D., *Beyond Death's Door* (New York, Bantam Books, 1979), p. 68. Used by permission.

Linda, a nurse who has worked with many terminal patients, shares the same insight:

I worked on the oncology floor, and sometimes we would lose four patients in one day. When I worked in a nursing home, I have seen people whose family had left them there to die; in one case they had gone on a cruise and had already made the arrangements.

I remember one older lady who would ask me to phone her husband to come sit with her through the night because she was afraid it would be that night.

Most of these people—some of them very old—didn't experience pain except in certain situations. It was an easing out of this life and into another.

I remember one man we were with recently. For the last half hour we just sat with him and held his hand and watched to see if he needed anything. When it came it was like taking a sigh or like a restful last breath.

The Startling New Testament Attitude
Toward Death

Nowhere else is there anything like the New Testament attitude toward death. Nothing in Oriental religions, nothing in mysticism, nothing in Judaism or Islam. Nothing in thanatology, in existentialism, or in the cults.

Reading Psalm 23 we say to ourselves, "That's the way I feel. If I have to walk through the valley of the shadow of death I will, and I'll try not to be afraid because I know God is with me. But I'd rather stay here."

Paul's attitude was almost the opposite. If you paraphrase Philippians 1:23, you can hear Paul saying something like this: "If I have to stay here, I will; but I'd rather depart and be with Christ, which is a lot better."

Being with Christ must really be something! Better than travel? Yes, better. Better than preaching? You don't like to preach, Paul? Yes, I love to preach, but being with Christ would be better. In fact, I am ready to go. "For to me, to live is Christ and to die is gain" (Philippians 1:21).

In 2 Corinthians 5:1-10, Paul contrasts this life and the life to come, the earthly and the Heavenly. He has a special reason for using *tent* to illustrate what he means, for Corinth was one place where he worked as a tentmaker. Aquila and Priscilla were his fellow workers (Acts 18:1-3).

We think of tents as only for camping or the Boy Scouts, but in Paul's day some people lived in them! Today in the Middle East you can still see nomads living in tents.

Paul knew what it was to make a new tent to replace one that had worn out through use, and he saw that as an example of the way our bodies wear out and die. But instead of only another tent, subject to the same weakness and death, God will give us a permanent home, one that will last through eternity.

Life is temporary; life is also incomplete. You win the game, and everybody cheers. Then what? You sweat and work and finally achieve your objective, but what for? You get a job, do your best, but somehow you are not quite happy. You go to another job, but before long that one too isn't quite all you expected.

In this life, like Paul, "we groan and are burdened," yearning for that perfect place.

Are we wrong in this? Is our disappointment only selfish pessimism? Oh, no. God "has made us for this very purpose and has given us the Spirit as a deposit, guaranteeing what is to come" (2 Corinthians 5:5). Our yearning will be fulfilled in that life to come, and only then.

We're seeing new faces in our country, faces from Europe, faces from Asia, faces from Latin America. We think of them as foreigners. Maybe we should remember that we Christians are foreigners and strangers in this world (1 Peter 2:11). We don't really belong here.

We forget that we are sojourners, pilgrims, tenants. We have become settlers. We act as if we're here to stay! We put down roots and make our plans and live as if we have a permanent title to the air above us and the earth beneath us.

We think about this life and things to eat and wear and drive. We concentrate upon the here and now, forgetting so often about the world to come. We have it all backwards.

Faced with the fact of mortality, we choose not to think about it at all. "Later," we tell ourselves, and hurry back to whatever it was we were doing before this troublesome thought intruded.

But our citizenship is in heaven. And we eagerly await a Savior from there, the Lord Jesus Christ, who, by the power that enables him to bring everything under his control, will transform our lowly bodies so that they will be like his glorious body.

—Philippians 3:20, 21

Think It Over

1. Since our citizenship is in Heaven, what are we to do about getting a job, buying property, setting goals, making plans?

2. How do you react to this statement: To face death you must first face life?

3. Describe present attitudes among Christians as compared or contrasted to the attitude in 2 Corinthians 5:1-10.

If a man dies, will he live again?
                    —Job

Does the Old Testament Teach Life After Death?

What does the Old Testament say about life after death? The pathetic lament in Ecclesiastes 3 doesn't sound too encouraging:

> I also thought, "... Man's fate is like that of the animals; the same fate awaits them both: As one dies, so dies the other. All have the same breath; man has no advantage over the animal. Everything is meaningless."
>   —Ecclesiastes 3:18, 19

Standing over the still and silent form of his brother, did Cain ask, "What happened? Where did Abel go? Is he coming back?"

The Case of Job
Whether or not Cain wondered about life after death we don't know, but we know one who did: Job, whose struggles are told so dramatically in that sobbing chronicle that bears his name.

"If a man dies," Job cried, "will he live again?"

No wonder Job asked that question. Rich, secure, with his family nearby, Job saw it all taken away in one tragedy after another. Rustlers, lightning, and tornado robbed him of riches and children. Nor did his troubles stop there. Painful, disfiguring sores broke out all over his body.

His wife made things worse by her attitude, and when three friends came to sympathize, Job probably wished they would keep their mouths shut. They kept insinuating that it was all Job's fault, that his misfortunes were due to some sin or sins he was committing.

Possessions gone, family dead, Job rubbed his itching sores with a broken piece of pottery and wished he were dead.

> "Why did I not perish at birth,
> and die as I came from the womb?"
> —Job 3:11

Job sought release, rest, peace, even death; anything to escape his suffering. The grave began to look good to him.

> There the wicked cease from turmoil,
> and there the weary are at rest.
> Captives also enjoy their ease;
> they no longer hear the slave driver's shout.
> The small and the great are there,
> and the slave is freed from his master.
> —Job 3:17-19

Forcing him to think about life and death, Job's troubles made him aware of how short life really is. Sometimes when he thought of death there surged up within him a feeling of helplessness, of hopelessness. He could hardly stand to think about it.

> My days are swifter than a weaver's shuttle,
> and they come to an end without hope.
> Remember, O God, that my life is but a breath;
> my eyes will never see happiness again.
> . . . .
> As a cloud vanishes and is gone,
> so he who goes down to the grave does not return.
> He will never come to his house again;
> his place will know him no more.
> —Job 7:6-10

Everything seemed so dark to Job, so uncertain—everything except the relentless approach of death. Hear his despairing plea:

Are not my few days almost over?
Turn away from me so I can have a moment's joy
before I go to the place of no return.
—Job 10:20, 21

Was it possible that a person could live after death? Job yearned to know. Could there be a future beyond the grave, an unknown

---

*Death has climbed in through our windows and
has entered our fortresses.*

—Jeremiah 9:21

---

world out there somewhere? The question kept coming back to Job again and again. Even in his misery he found a gleam of hope in the Creator's care.

If a man dies, will he live again?
All the days of my hard service
I will wait for my renewal to come.
You will call and I will answer you;
you will long for the creature your hands have made.
—Job 14:14, 15

Yes, it seemed possible, even likely. If only he could be certain! The one thing that did seem certain was his death, and that could not be far away.

Only a few years will pass
before I go on the journey of no return.
My spirit is broken,
my days are cut short
the grave awaits me.
—Job 16:22—17:1

But was death the end? No. Job knew there was another world. There was another life. The God who had carried him through this life was not helpless—as man is—before onrushing death. God would still be with him, whether in this life or in that unmapped and unknown future. So from the depth of his misery we hear a shout that sounds triumphant:

I know that my Redeemer lives,
  and that in the end he will stand upon the earth.
And after my skin has been destroyed,
  yet in my flesh I will see God;
I myself will see him
  with my own eyes—I, and not another.
  How my heart yearns within me!

—Job 19:25-27

The Book of Ecclesiastes

Let's probe into another Old Testament book. Remember that dismal lament from Ecclesiastes quoted above? Much of the book is about the same.

"Meaningless! Meaningless!"
  says the Teacher.
"Utterly meaningless!
  Everything is meaningless!"
  —Ecclesiastes 1:2

Evidence indicates that Solomon wrote Ecclesiastes. The wisest man of his time, Solomon became a tragic figure in the end. Power, riches, and women—especially the latter—drew him away from God, and 1 Kings 11:9 sadly relates, "The Lord became angry with Solomon because his heart had turned away."

Contrast Solomon's decline with the career of Paul, apostle of Jesus Christ. The longer Paul lived, the closer he walked with God. Just the reverse was true with Solomon.

As Solomon thought about his life and coming death, and that he would one day have to leave all his wealth and splendor, he sank into near despair. He admitted that he hated life (Ecclesiastes 2:17), and he found little comfort in thinking about the life to come. "Who knows," he asked, "if the spirit of man rises upward and if the spirit of the animal goes down into the earth?" (Ecclesiastes 3:21).

When the Queen of Sheba came for an audience with Solomon, she was almost ecstatic. "How happy your men must be! How happy your officials, who continually stand before you and hear your wisdom" (2 Chronicles 9:7).

Was it by reciting such lines as the following that Solomon made her so enthusiastic? They probably had not been written yet. Let's look at them:

I declared that the dead,
  who had already died,
are happier than the living,
  who are still alive.
But better than both
  is he who has not yet been,
who has not seen the evil
  that is done under the sun.
          —Ecclesiastes 4:2, 3

We can almost visualize Solomon's head shaking as he talks about how sad it is that the dead are gone from this world and that "never again will they have a part in anything that happens under the sun" (Ecclesiastes 9:6).

Because of his attitude toward death, Solomon said that a person ought to try to pack as much as he or she can into this life, because, in his view, who knows what will come afterward?

Whatever your hand finds to do, do it with all your might, for in the grave, where you are going, there is neither working nor planning nor knowledge nor wisdom.
          —Ecclesiastes 9:10

Paul said it quite differently. He begins with almost the same words, but look at his conclusion!

Whatever you do, work at it with all your heart, as working for the Lord, not for men, since you know that you will receive an inheritance from the Lord as a reward.
          —Colossians 3:23, 24

In closing Solomon speaks of God's judgment, then offers his conclusions after he has examined life, death, and hereafter.

Remember your Creator
  in the days of your youth. . . .
before the pitcher is shattered at the spring,
  or the wheel is broken at the well,
and the dust returns to the ground it came from,
  and the spirit returns to God who gave it.
          —Ecclesiastes 12:1, 6, 7

The Psalms

The psalms contain many references to the grave, to dying, to death, and to what follows. Sometimes the writer means only what we mean when we say, "He is no longer living," or "He is gone." These are not statements about our belief or disbelief in a life to come; we are merely saying that the person is dead.

For example, in Psalm 90:5, Moses is not teaching "soul-sleeping"; he is contrasting man's brief life with God's eternal nature. Nor is David, in Psalm 31:17, predicting that sinners, after death, will be condemned eternally to silence in Sheol. He is reacting to the slander and conspiracy of his enemies (see verse 13), which will be silenced when they die. Such statements do not affirm life after death, nor do they deny it. They simply are not speaking on that subject, and we must look elsewhere for information about it.

Some references, such as Psalm 49:10-12, tell of death's finality, reminding us that death will cut short our plans and take us from the activities of this life. Others tell of death's inevitability (Psalm 89:48); of man's dread of death (Psalm 55:4). We recognize all those things, but none of them show that we either shall or shall not live after we die.

Many psalms tell of God's answers to prayers for deliverance and of how He has saved from death (Psalms 18:4-6; 30:3; 33:18, 19; 56:13; 86:13; 103:4; 107:17-20; 116:3-9; 138:7; and others). In many of these the thought is merely that of life preserved on earth for a time.

Sometimes psalmists ask for the death of their enemies, as in Psalm 58:6-8. This is a call for justice, however, not just a plea for personal revenge.

Woven throughout the

> **For Further Research**
> Compare and contrast these attitudes and events.
>
> 1. Solomon's career and Paul's experiences:
> 2 Chronicles 8 and 9
> 2 Corinthians 11:23–12:10
>
> 2. Solomon's outlook contrasted with Paul's:
> Ecclesiastes 12:8
> Philippians 1:21
>
> 3. David's attitude toward his enemies, Stephen's toward his murderers, Paul's toward his opponents:
> Psalm 55:15
> Acts 7:60
> Romans 10:1; Acts 26:29
>
> 4. God's question in Job 38:17 and Jesus' words in Revelation 1:18.

psalms is a conviction that God rewards the righteous with long life and good things, and that He will preserve them from death.

> He who dwells in the shelter of the Most High
> will rest in the shadow of the Almighty.
>
> . . . .
>
> "Because he loves me," says the Lord,
> "I will rescue him."
>
> . . . .
>
> "With long life will I satisfy him
> and show him my salvation."
> —Psalm 91:1, 14, 16

A psalm may speak of God's blessings here on earth, and say little about the life to come. See Psalm 1, Psalm 112, or Psalm 121. Does this show denial of eternity and the life to come? Hardly.

We Christians also are concerned about present welfare, though we are assured of eternal life. We ask God for healing, for protection, for life when death seems near, even though we cherish Jesus' promise, "Because I live, you also will live" (John 14:19). We are interested both in earthly welfare and in eternal welfare, and so were the psalmists.

Isaiah's statement in Isaiah 3:10 may have an earthly or a Heavenly meaning or both, but Asaph's confidence expressed in Psalm 73 cannot be limited to this world and this earthly life only. He is looking into the next life and the next world.

Neither the sun nor death can be looked at steadily.
—Francois Duc de La Rochefoucauld

> Yet I am always with you;
> you hold me by my right hand.
> You guide me with your counsel,
> and afterward you will take me into glory.
> Whom have I in heaven but you?
> And being with you, I desire nothing on earth.
> My flesh and my heart may fail,
> but God is the strength of my heart
> and my portion forever.
> —Psalm 73:23-26

The Sons of Korah, in Psalm 49, recognize that "wise men die; the foolish and the senseless alike perish and leave their wealth to others," but they go on to say, "God will redeem my soul from the grave; he will surely take me to himself" (verses 10 and 15).

It is no accident that David's Shepherd Psalm has been the favorite of millions. These verses speak to the heart.

> The Lord is my shepherd, I shall lack nothing.
> He makes me lie down in green pastures,
> he leads me beside quiet waters,
> he restores my soul.
> He guides me in paths of righteousness
> for his name's sake.
> Even though I walk
> through the valley of the shadow of death,
> I will fear no evil,
> for you are with me;
> your rod and your staff,
> they comfort me.
>
> You prepare a table before me
> in the presence of my enemies.
> You anoint my head with oil;
> my cup overflows.
> Surely goodness and love will follow me
> all the days of my life,
> and I will dwell in the house of the Lord
> forever.
>
> —Psalm 23

Can it be that David believed God's strong and gentle care would be abruptly cut off at the moment of death? If he did, why would he speak of "walking through" rather than "lying down" in death's dark valley? If he did, why deliberately follow "all the days of my life" with "house of the Lord forever"?

Careful writer, David was expressing his complete trust in God's care both in this life and the next.

We see this again in Psalm 16, which Peter quotes in Acts 2 as a prediction of Jesus' resurrection. Yes, Jesus would be the "firstfruits" (1 Corinthians 15:20-23), but did not David, guided by the Holy Spirit, foresee also his own resurrection and ours?

I have set the Lord always before me.
   Because he is at my right hand,
   I will not be shaken.
Therefore my heart is glad and my tongue rejoices;
   my body also will rest secure,
because you will not abandon me to the grave,
   nor will you let your Holy One see decay.
You have made known to me the path of life;
   you will fill me with joy in your presence,
   with eternal pleasures at your right hand.
                                    —Psalm 16:8-11

Elsewhere in the Old Testament
Isaiah foresaw a time when God would remove "the shroud that
enfolds all peoples." No wonder Paul referred to this prediction in
that great chapter on the resurrection (1 Corinthians 15:54).

   On this mountain the Lord Almighty will prepare
      a feast of rich food for all peoples,
   a banquet of aged wine—
      the best of meats and the finest of wines.
   On this mountain he will destroy
      the shroud that enfolds all peoples,
   the sheet that covers all nations;
      he will swallow up death forever.
   The Sovereign Lord will wipe away the tears
      from all faces;
   he will remove the disgrace of his people
      from all the earth.

                                    —Isaiah 25:6-8

John would not write of "the wedding supper of the Lamb" (Revelation 19:9) until eight hundred years later; but here in Israel's de-
clining years as a nation, Isaiah looked ahead and saw the same
future John described:

   Now the dwelling of God is with men, and he will live with
   them. They will be his people, and God himself will be with
   them and be their God. He will wipe every tear from their
   eyes. There will be no more death.

                                    —Revelation 21:3, 4

The prophet Hosea, who lived about the same time as Isaiah, issued God's appeal, calling his people back from idolatry as a husband would implore a wayward wife to come home. Hidden among God's repeated invitations are four lines so important and vivid that Paul uses them also in 1 Corinthians 15:

> I will ransom them from the power of the grave;
> I will redeem them from death.
> Where, O death, are your plagues?
> Where, O grave, is your destruction?
> —Hosea 13:14

Daniel wrote about kingdoms and rulers and empires. But Daniel also had a vision of a kingdom that would transcend time, a Kingdom that would be eternal.

> The saints of the Most High will receive the kingdom and will possess it forever—yes, for ever and ever.
> —Daniel 7:18

He wrote of great distress coming within the kingdoms of men and then, in clear and unmistakable terms, wrote of the coming resurrection of the dead:

> At that time Michael, the great prince who protects your people, will arise. There will be a time of distress such as has not happened from the beginning of nations until then. But at that time your people—everyone whose name is found written in the book—will be delivered. Multitudes who sleep in the dust of the earth will awake: some to everlasting life, others to shame and everlasting contempt.
> —Daniel 12:1, 2

Demonstrations of a Life After This One

It is well known that several resurrections from the dead are recorded in the New Testament. What is not so widely known is that this occurs in the Old Testament also.

The books of 1 and 2 Kings are not poetry, as is Psalms, nor philosophical reflection, as is Ecclesiastes. These are the national archives, the official history, and both 1 Kings and 2 Kings tell of persons being brought back from the dead.

In 1 Kings 17:21-24, we read that the prophet Elijah cried out to God for the life of a dead boy, the son of a widow who had helped Elijah during a long famine, and God answered Elijah's prayer by restoring the boy to life.

When Elijah finished his career, Elisha was chosen to succeed him. The child of a couple in Shunem died, and the mother immediately went to find Elisha. Had she heard what his predecessor had done in the case of the widow's son?

The woman came to Elisha, who sent his servant, Gehazi, to lay Elisha's staff on the dead boy's face. Gehazi did so, but nothing happened.

---

*The whole of his life had prepared
Podduyev for living, not for dying.
—Solzhenitsyn, in* Cancer Ward

When Elisha reached the house, there was the boy lying dead on his couch. He went in, shut the door on the two of them and prayed unto the Lord. Then he got on the bed and lay upon the boy, mouth to mouth, eyes to eyes, hands to hands. As he stretched himself out upon him, the boy's body grew warm. Elisha turned away and walked back and forth in the room and then got on the bed and stretched out upon him once more. The boy sneezed seven times and opened his eyes.

Elisha summoned Gehazi and said, "Call the Shunammite." And he did. When she came, he said, "Take your son." She came in, fell at his feet and bowed to the ground. Then she took her son and went out.

—2 Kings 4:32-37

Sounds like a paramedic doing CPR, doesn't it? We might be tempted to settle for that explanation in this case, but not in the case of the dead man who came to life again when his body was thrown into Elisha's tomb and touched the prophet's bones (2 Kings 13:21). There is no question about it: history records that dead people have lived again.

Elisha was witness to an event so extraordinary that it only happened one other time in history. On Elijah's last day on earth, he and Elisha were walking together.

As they were walking along and talking together, suddenly a chariot of fire and horses of fire appeared and separated the two of them, and Elijah went up to heaven in a whirlwind. Elisha saw this and cried out, "My father! My father! The chariots and horsemen of Israel!" And Elisha saw him no more.

—2 Kings 2:11, 12

The only other person we know of who did not die but went from this life directly into the next was Enoch. Hebrews 11 numbers him among the heroes of the faith.

By faith Enoch was taken from this life, so that he did not experience death; he could not be found, because God had taken him away. For before he was taken, he was commended as one who pleased God. —Hebrews 11:5

Enoch pleased God by walking with Him: that is, by worshiping and obeying Him. The record goes on to say this:

Altogether, Enoch lived 365 years. Enoch walked with God; then he was no more, because God took him away.

—Genesis 5:23, 24

If there were no life beyond this earth, then what Enoch received for walking with God would be punishment rather than reward. His life was cut short. He lived on earth only 365 years. His father lived 962 years, and his son lived 969. But Enoch was rewarded by being taken from his short life on earth to eternal life in Heaven.

Conclusions From Our Study

Does the Old Testament teach life after death? Definitely it does, through history and poetry and prophecy. Dead people were brought back, not as disembodied spirits but as the same persons they were before, recognized and known by those closest to them. Enoch and Elijah did not die at all, but went directly into another world, still living, still themselves. David looked forward to life in the house of the Lord forever.

Is there any possibility that our findings are only wishful thinking, that we have somehow missed the meaning of the various passages we've looked at? Hear Jesus. He believed that life after death was taught in the Old Testament.

When the disbelieving Sadducees came to question Him, He turned them back to their own Scriptures, referring to God's call to Moses from the burning bush:

> But in the account of the bush, even Moses showed that the dead rise, for he calls the Lord "the God of Abraham, and the God of Isaac, and the God of Jacob." He is not the God of the dead, but of the living, for to him all are alive.
>
> —Luke 20:37, 38

Think It Over

1. First Samuel 28 describes a strange incident that gives its own forceful evidence that life continues beyond death. Check into it and see what you think.

2. David's obituary is found in 1 Chronicles 29:28; Paul's in 2 Timothy 4:6-8. What is your reaction as you compare them?

3. Compare the raising of Dorcas (Acts 9:36-42) and Eutychus (Acts 20:7-12) with those in 1 Kings 17:17-24 and 2 Kings 4:32-37. Are there differences? Are there similarities?

No, I have never been there. But I have a very
dear Friend who has been there—Jesus Christ.
                            —*Dr. Ross H. Stover*[1]

Jesus Comes Back From the Dead

One of the most powerful speeches ever delivered came from
Winston Churchill on Monday, May 13, 1940, to the House of
Commons. Hitler's troops had invaded Poland September 1 of the
previous year, unleashing the chaos of World War II, and the government of Prime Minister Neville Chamberlain had fallen. King
George VI had asked Churchill to form a government, and Churchill
had convened the House, asking for a vote of confidence in his new
administration. Seldom has there been a crisis more fearful, and
seldom has an audience listened more attentively. The very life of
the nation was at stake.

Churchill reported his progress in filling the various offices in the
government, then added, "I have nothing to offer but blood, toil,
tears, and sweat."

He ended his address by reminding the House of their ultimate
goal: "You ask, What is our aim? I can answer in one word: Victory—
victory at all costs, victory in spite of all terror; victory, however long
and hard the road may be."[2]

---

1. Quoted by Maurice Rawlings, M.D., *Beyond Death's Door* (New York, Bantam Books,
1979), p. 37.

2. Winston S. Churchill, *Their Finest Hour* (New York, Bantam Books, 1962), p. 22.

The House unanimously gave Churchill their approval, and Britain went on to see the victory Churchill predicted. Churchill's defiance of Nazism forms one of the brightest pages of all history, yet this great man suffered defeat from an enemy he could not overcome. A reporter tells of seeing Churchill late in the old man's life.

I was in the visitor's gallery of the House of Commons when Sir Winston unexpectedly appeared on the floor. There was a hush as the old man waddled feebly toward his accustomed seat, hunched over and uncertain of every step. He sat down heavily and looked around the House, owlishly, unseeing, as if for some long-vanished familiar face, and then, as the debate resumed, his big head slumped forward grotesquely on his chest. He was an empty husk of a man, all the wit and elegance and greatness drained out of him by age.[3]

A year or so after that, Churchill succumbed to death's relentless encroachment. How tragic to read of the decline and death of someone like this, whose personal strength and resolution held his nation together and led them to great heights! But death came. Death ended the dream. Death had the last word.

Like water spilled on the ground, which cannot be recovered, so we must die.
—The Woman of Tekoa

How different in the case of Jesus! After His enemies had done their worst, after they had nailed Him to a cross and watched Him die, after they had stationed a squad of soldiers around His tomb, He tore away every barrier and came back from the dead.

Was His an "out of the body" experience like some you read about? For example, consider this one:

It was about two years ago, and I had just turned nineteen. I was driving a friend of mine home in my car, and as I got to this particular intersection downtown, I stopped and looked both ways, but I didn't see a thing coming. I pulled on out into the intersection and as I did I heard my friend yell at the top of

---

3. Stewart Alsop, *Stay of Execution* (Philadelphia, J. B. Lippincott Company, 1973), p. 290.

his voice. When I looked I saw a blinding light, the headlights of a car that was speeding toward us. I heard this awful sound—the side of the car being crushed in—and there was just an instant during which I seemed to be going through a darkness, an enclosed space. It was very quick. Then, I was sort of floating about five feet above the street, about five yards away from the car, I'd say, and I heard the echo of the crash dying away. I saw people come running up and crowding around the car, and I saw my friend get out of the car, obviously in shock. I could see my own body in the wreckage among all those people, and could see them trying to get it out. My legs were all twisted and there was blood all over the place.[4]

Dr. Raymond A. Moody, Jr., who reported this account from the young man who "died" in the automobile accident, tells of similar recollections from persons who were near death or had been pronounced dead. Dr. Moody believes that recent advances in resuscitation techniques are responsible for saving many who otherwise would have died and may account for the seeming increase in these experiences.

One such experience is mentioned in chapter 4 of this book. (See page 40.) A man who was struck by lightning later reported that he felt good while attendants were trying to restore him to life. In fact, he was so well pleased with his condition that he resented their efforts. He was thinking, "What are they doing? Why don't they leave me dead?"

Dr. Moody mentions that he has found cases in which resuscitation took place as long as twenty minutes with no evidence of brain damage, although medical personnel are generally agreed that resuscitation should not be attempted longer than five minutes because in most instances by that time irreversible brain damage will have taken place.

Five minutes? Fifteen? Twenty minutes? People can "come back" after being "dead" as long as twenty minutes?

What about three days? Was Jesus' resurrection another of those "near death" experiences where CPR methods restore heartbeat and respiration? Let's look at the records and see what did happen.

---

4. Raymond A. Moody, Jr., *Life After Life and Reflections on Life After Life* (Guideposts Mockingbird Books, Covington, Georgia, 1975), p. 27. Used by permission.

Jesus' Death
John 19:28-42

Fortunately, we have the record of an eyewitness. The apostle John, probably one of the very first to follow Jesus (John 1:35-40; 21:24), stayed closer than any of the others during Jesus' trial (John 18:15), and was with Jesus even at the cross (John 19:25-27). We are indebted to John for his detailed report.

The victim of a crucifixion faced two opposing and intolerable circumstances. His weight was supported by nails through his hands, so that as he hung suspended his chest was constricted until he could hardly breathe. When he just had to have some air, he would struggle upward, pressing against the nail or nails in his feet, and quickly fill his lungs several times until the pain became so intense that he had to give up and sink down again. This was repeated over and over.

If his executioners wanted to hurry the proceedings they took a club and smashed his thigh bones, making it impossible for him to use his legs to obtain even this small relief. Death came much quicker then.

John was there when Jesus died. After the soldiers had broken the legs of the first thief, John watched as they came to Jesus. They noticed that He was dead and, just to make sure, one of them took his spear and rammed it upward underneath the ribs toward the heart. From where he stood John saw the flow of blood and water when the soldier withdrew the spear.

Joseph of Arimathea asked Pilate for the body, and Nicodemus, who had come to Jesus one night about three years earlier (John 3), purchased a quantity of spices and ointments for the burial.

Hurrying, because at sundown the Sabbath began, they laid Jesus' body in Joseph's own nearby tomb. Hesitant while Jesus was alive to take a stand for Him, Joseph wanted to do something now (John 19:38).

Responding to a warning from the chief priests and the Pharisees that Jesus said He would rise again, Pilate ordered the tomb to be sealed and a guard posted (Matthew 27:62-66).

Jesus Comes Back From the Dead
John 20:1-9

The feast of Passover had brought thousands to Jerusalem. Jesus' disciples, many from Galilee, were dispersed across the city wherever they could find lodging. The Sabbath had ended at sundown the previous day. Several women wanted to add their offering of spices and ointments to those Nicodemus had provided. They planned to be at the tomb as early as possible Sunday morning.

It was still dark when Mary Magdalene, Mary the mother of James, and Salome (Mark 16:1), left to go to the tomb. With them were Joanna and some others (Luke 24:10). Apparently they had some distance to go, and arrived at sunrise (Mark 16:2). As they went, they wondered how they would move the stone away from the entrance (Mark 16:3).

But God's angel had already moved it (Matthew 28:1-4), and Jesus had risen. Mary, perhaps hurrying ahead of the others, found to her astonishment that it was empty. Not even waiting to talk with the other women, she ran to the place Peter and John were staying to tell them that someone had taken the body.

The other women went inside the empty tomb. Just then two angels appeared. "Why do you look for the living among the dead?" they asked. "He is not here; he has risen" (Luke 24:5, 6).

Meanwhile Mary found Peter and John, who came running to the tomb. John, probably younger, reached it first. He didn't go inside; but Peter, when he came, went on in. The burial clothes were still there, and the head covering, but where was the body?

John, hesitant at first, now went into the sepulchre. When he saw the head covering neatly folded and the wrappings undisturbed but with no body inside, suddenly realization dawned. Jesus had walked out of His grave! Some students think John at this time believed only what Mary had told him—that the body was gone. But it seems rather that this "disciple whom Jesus loved" was ahead of the rest. He believed that Jesus had risen!

Repeatedly Jesus had told the disciples that He would rise from the dead. (See "For Further Research.") They had not accepted that prediction because they had refused to believe that He would die (Matthew 16:21, 22). They thought the Messiah must live and rule for ever (Isaiah 9:6, 7). Apparently they supposed He was using figurative language that they did not understand (Mark 9:10). Their dullness—especially in the light of their proximity to Him—cautions against a know-it-all attitude on our part.

The Old Testament predicted the Messiah's reign on David's throne. Could Jesus' brief popularity fulfill such promises of unending power and glory? If Jesus was the Messiah—and John and the others had been sure of that—this could not be the end. Jesus *had* to rise again.

Jesus Appears to Mary Magdalene
John 20:10-18

The Gospels do not hide the disciples' confusion. These puzzled men don't know what to do, don't know what to think. Before they have had time to recover from their grief and shock at Jesus' awful death, they find the tomb opened and the body gone. Now what?

Peter and John go back to their lodging place. When Mary comes again to the tomb, weary no doubt after running to get them and then trying to keep up with them on the way back, the two men are already gone.

What next? No wonder she stands there crying. Looking into the tomb again, she sees an angel sitting where Jesus' head had been, and another angel at the foot of His resting place.

The term *woman* sounds almost rude in our language, but in that time and place it was a respectful address. "Woman, why are you crying?" the angels ask. Why? First they have killed her Friend, then they have plundered His grave and stolen His body.

Jesus has come up behind her. "Woman," He says, "why are you crying? Who is it you are looking for?" (John 20:15).

Mary thinks He is the caretaker. Who else would be there? "Sir, if you have carried him away, tell me where you have put him, and I will get him" (John 20:15).

One word changes everything: "Mary." She turns to face Him and cries out, "Teacher!"

He's alive! He was dead and now He's alive! It's Jesus, alive again!

"Do not hold on to me," Jesus tells her, "for I have not yet returned to the Father. Go instead to my brothers and tell them, I am returning to my Father and your Father, to my God and your God" (John 20:17).

Mary leaves the tomb once more, but this time with a much different message. Now she can say, "I have seen the Lord, and He told me to tell you this."

For Further Research

Even Jesus' enemies knew He predicted He would rise again (Matthew 27:62-64). Look at these predictions—some nearly hidden but others very plain—and see what He said:

Matthew 12:38-40
Matthew 16:21
Matthew 20:18, 19
Matthew 26:31, 32
Mark 9:9, 10
Luke 18:31-34
John 2:19-22.

On the Road to Emmaus
Luke 24:13-35

Many people besides the twelve apostles were followers of Jesus. That day two of them left Jerusalem to go to Emmaus, a village about seven miles away. Probably they lived there. One of them was called Cleopas, and the other is not named.

As they went along, Jesus came and walked with them. Somehow He kept them from recognizing Him as He greeted them with a question that touched a sympathetic chord: "What are you discussing together as you walk along?"

They stopped, dejected, nearly crushed by the weight of sorrow that had fallen upon them. "Are you the only one living in Jerusalem," Cleopas asked, "who doesn't know the things that have happened there in these days?"

"What things?" Jesus asked; and the two men poured out their hearts, telling how their hopes were shattered when the chief priests and rulers succeeded in having Jesus sentenced to death and crucified.

One of the men told how the women had come back from the tomb saying the body was gone. Nor was that all.

> They came and told us that they had seen a vision of angels, who said he was alive. Then some of our companions went to the tomb and found it just as the women had said, but him they did not see.
>
> —Luke 24:23, 24

Not much later the same women were saying they had

For Further Research
Read about these appearances of Jesus after His resurrection.

- To Mary Magdalene, Mark 16:9, 10; John 20:11-18
- To the Women, Matthew 28:9, 10
- To Peter, 1 Corinthians 15:5; Luke 24:34
- On the Emmaus Road, Mark 16:12, 13; Luke 24:13-32
- To the Eleven, Mark 16:14, Luke 24:36-49; John 20:19-23
- To the Eleven a week later with Thomas present, John 20:24-29
- By the Sea, John 21:1-23
- To the Apostles and 500 others, Matthew 28:16-20; 1 Corinthians 15:6
- To James, 1 Corinthians 15:7
- Various times, Acts 1:3-5
- Final appearance and ascension, Mark 16:19; Luke 24:50-53; Acts 1:6-11

seen Jesus, but those two travelers had left too soon to hear that. They ended their report by saying, "Him they did not see." Vision or no vision, they knew Jesus was dead. See Him alive again?

Still Jesus did not let them know who He was. Instead, He led them through a brief survey of the predictions of His coming in the Old Testament. What a lesson! Think what it would be to have Christ personally explain the link between inspired prophecy and its fulfillment in His betrayal and trial and crucifixion, and in His burial and resurrection. Later the two men would recall how they felt in this unforgettable encounter (Luke 24:32).

As the three approached Emmaus, it seemed that Jesus was going farther. "Stay with us," they urged, "for it is nearly evening; the day is almost over" (Luke 24:29).

So Jesus went into the house with them. During supper He took bread and gave thanks and began to distribute it. All at once they recognized their guest. His task completed, Jesus disappeared.

Now we can see why Jesus did not let them recognize Him earlier. Had they known who He was, they would have been too excited to listen to His explanation of the Scriptures. They would have rushed back to Jerusalem to tell the other disciples.

Now they did rush back to Jerusalem, even though the day was nearly over. Quickly they found the place where some of Jesus' followers were together. They intended to tell the apostles that Jesus was alive again, but they found the apostles telling them!

"It is true! The Lord has risen and has appeared to Simon." Then Cleopas and his friend told the apostles how Jesus walked with them and what He said to them, and how they recognized Him.

Jesus Comes to His Disciples
John 20:19-23

The group's excited talk is interrupted when suddenly Jesus stands there in the room. How did He get there? The door is locked. The disciples think they must be seeing a ghost.

Jesus soon gets rid of that idea. He shows them His hands wounded by the nails. He urges them to put their hands on Him and know He is solid flesh and bone. He eats a piece of broiled fish (Luke 24:36-43). Ghosts do not eat solid food.

Jesus wanted them—and He wants us—to know that they were not imagining things. John's comment shows how he and the others felt, and how we would have felt had we been there: "The disciples were overjoyed when they saw the Lord" (John 20:20).

Jesus gives them the Holy Spirit, perhaps a foretaste of what will happen later on the Day of Pentecost (Acts 2), and tells them that He will send them out as His representatives. Guided by the Holy Spirit, the terms of forgiveness they will offer will be those God wants them to offer. Anyone refusing their divinely inspired mission will in reality be refusing God.

In the New Testament after the resurrection of our Lord there is from the lips of a believer scarcely a note of pessimism.

—Andrew W. Blackwood[5]

"Then he opened their minds so they could understand the Scriptures" (Luke 24:45). He explained the prophecies that He had explained to the two on the way to Emmaus. Earlier Jesus had promised the Holy Spirit to guide His apostles into all truth (John 16:13). When Jesus was no longer with them, the Spirit would be their guide, as we see in the second chapter of Acts. But now Jesus himself is opening their minds to the truth.

The first truth they must understand is that He is alive. Though He was dead, though He was buried, Jesus came to life again, is alive today, and will never die.

Thomas was not present when Jesus came that first Sunday evening. When the disciples told him they had seen Jesus, he refused to believe, just as the others had refused to believe the women who had seen Jesus first.

Jesus Convinces a Doubter
John 20:24-29

Thomas was a twin. Perhaps he knew what it was to be mistaken about identification. He had to be sure. "Unless I see the nail marks in his hands," Thomas declared, "and put my finger where the nails were, and put my hand into his side, I will not believe it" (John 20:25).

No one was going to fool Thomas.

A week later the disciples were meeting again, and this time Thomas was there. Jesus came into the room, stood there and of-

---

5. From *The Funeral* by Andrew Watterson Blackwood, Copyright by Baker Book House. Used by permission of Baker Book Houser.

fered Thomas the opportunity to see for himself: "Put your finger here; see my hands. Reach out your hand and put it into my side. Stop doubting and believe" (John 20:27).

Thomas' doubts lasted longer than the others', but now his response is no less positive. Seeing Jesus, and knowing the report is true, Thomas cries, "My Lord and my God!" (John 20:28).

We can be glad Thomas asked for proof. He saw and was convinced. Though we haven't seen, his experience strengthens our belief. Jesus referred to us when He told Thomas, "Because you have seen me, you have believed; blessed are those who have not seen and yet have believed" (John 20:29).

Why the Gospels Were Written
John 20:30, 31

John summarizes the reason he wrote his Gospel, and his statement can be taken for the books by Matthew, Mark, and Luke as well. None of them wrote everything Jesus did. Each one gave us just a few examples from His life. All four tell us of Jesus' resurrection.

Though the four Gospels present only a portion of the evidence, in this brief chapter we have not even considered all they tell us. We have not touched on Jesus' appearance by the Sea of Galilee (John 21), nor His Great Commission to His disciples to go out and tell the world (Matthew 28:16-20). But hear what John says:

> Jesus did many other miraculous signs in the presence of his disciples, which are not recorded in this book. But these are written that you may believe that Jesus is the Christ, the Son of God, and that by believing you may have life in his name.
>
> —John 20:30, 31

Think It Over

1. Everybody knows that people don't come back to life after they are dead and buried; yet we have four records, written near the time and place where it happened, telling us that Jesus did come back. What are your thoughts about this?

2. Suppose Jesus' enemies had succeeded in killing Him and sealing His body in a tomb forever. What would that tell you?

3. Would you agree or disagree with this statement: "I don't believe the resurrection is important. Jesus' teaching and example are what counts."

*No one writing a fairy tale could ever have
been satisfied with such meager and
matter-of-fact details.*

— *R.C. Foster*[1]

Jesus' Resurrection: Can We Be Sure?

Do you go to cemeteries very often? There's one here in town
where you can find as many joggers as dead people. Well, almost as
many. Not quite as many. Nowhere near as many. Maybe half a
dozen. Or three or four. Sometimes only me. But some people do go
to cemeteries to jog, or to enjoy the stillness, or to see the trees and
flowers. But the usual reason is none of these.

Most people go to graveyards to pay their respects to those whose
bodies lie buried there. I remember rounding a bend late one afternoon and coming upon a young man bending over a freshly made
grave. Hoping he had not seen me, I changed direction and headed
down another way. When I came back he was gone.

I couldn't help going over to see.

At the foot of the grave, almost buried by the wilted flowers, was a
little metal stand holding a cardboard marker with the name and
date. The body was that of a girl, probably his wife, twenty-two,
buried less than three weeks.

Yes, people return to the burial places of their loved ones so they
can feel close to them.

---

1. From *The Final Week* by R.C. Foster, Copyright 1962 by Baker Book House. Used by
permission of Baker Book House.

In Jesus' case this is impossible.

His body isn't here. You can't go to the place where His body is buried. It isn't here.

Did you get that?

Jesus' tomb is empty.

The body is gone.

Where Did the Body Go?

Jesus was not tried in secret and shot in a cellar. His trial was a noisy affair, with shouted accusations, a crowd, soldiers, a lengthy procession to the place of execution, and death not coming until long hours of public exposure and shame.

On Pentecost when Peter spoke of Jesus' trial and crucifixion, no one had to ask, "Which Jesus?" Everybody knew.

His death was public; His burial scarcely less so.

Joseph of Arimathea was a rich and prominent member of the Sanhedrin, respected as "a good and upright man" (Luke 23:50). Nicodemus, too, was a member of this ruling body (John 7:50).

Here were two of the nation's leaders, comparable to our Senators, perhaps, claiming the body from Governor Pilate. Surprised that Jesus had died so soon, Pilate sent for the centurion and questioned him to be sure (Mark 15:44).

No ordinary grave for Jesus. Joseph placed the body in his own new tomb, the one he had commissioned to be chiseled out of solid

---

Pierre is sleeping in his last sleep beneath the earth; it is the end of everything, everything, everything.

*-Madame Curie, in her
diary, after her husband's tragic death*

---

rock. Only the rich could afford such. The tomb had only recently been completed and fortunately was close to the place of death (John 19:41).

Neither man spared expense. For burial wrapping, Joseph bought linen. Nicodemus' contribution was a hundred *litrai* (about seventy-five pounds) of myrrh and aloes to be placed about the body.

"The women," Luke tells us, "who had come with Jesus from Galilee followed Joseph and saw the tomb and how his body was laid in it" (Luke 23:55). Their closest friend was being laid to rest, and they had to see the place.

Nor were they the only ones interested in the proceedings. Remembering what Jesus had said, His accusers went to Pilate and arranged for a guard to be posted. Taking no chances, the soldiers secured the tomb and placed their seal on the stone door (Matthew 27:62-66). Can you think of any better way to make sure the body would *not* be stolen?

Before dawn on Sunday morning the women came to add their spices to those Nicodemus had provided. The events of that morning have been repeated to us so often that it is difficult for us to grasp their stunned reaction at finding the tomb opened and empty.

Mary runs to Peter and John. The other women see an angel, who tells them Jesus is risen. With mixed feelings of fear and joy, they hurry off to tell the disciples.

Peter and John come running, John reaching the tomb first. He looks in but stands outside. Then Peter comes and goes on in, and John follows.

By now the terror-stricken guards have reached the authorities, setting off another reaction. The authorities hold a conference and put out a cover story.

Reports begin to come that different ones have seen Jesus: Mary Magdalene, some other women, Simon Peter. It is a bewildered group that comes together that evening, made even more bewildered when the men from Emmaus burst in, saying they have seen Him and He has gone home with them.

First Accusation: The Disciples Stole the Body

Search carefully. Go back over every inch of ground; dissect every conversation. Whatever else the disciples are doing, they're not sitting around saying, "Hey, guys, what do we do with this body we stole?"

Yet this is precisely what they were accused of doing.

> When the chief priests had met with the elders and devised a plan, they gave the soldiers a large sum of money, telling them, "You are to say, 'His disciples came during the night and stole him away while we were asleep.' If this report gets to the governor, we will satisfy him and keep you out of trouble." So the soldiers took the money and did as they were instructed. And this story has been widely circulated among the Jews to this very day.
>
> —Matthew 28:12-15

How did the disciples get away with that body? Did all eleven help with it? Or was it supposed that only one or two did the deed?

Did Peter take Jesus' body? That coward! He was so afraid that he let a little servant girl scare a denial out of him. Would stealing have given him the courage to stand before a crowd and announce that Jesus had risen from the dead? And do it so effectively that three thousand were convinced and turned to Christ?

Did Thomas? Doubter, a twin, knowing how people could mistake identity. Okay, Thomas, suppose you stole the body. What for? So you could be sure you knew where Jesus was? Then what? You wouldn't believe even when they started telling you that He had come back. Would you have let them go on saying He was alive if you knew He was still dead?

Maybe John took the body. John stayed closest when Jesus was on trial, closest when He was on the cross. Maybe John couldn't think of parting with Jesus and crept past the guards, forced the door open, shouldered the body onto his back and struggled off with it.

Where would he take it? He had no home in Jerusalem: he was a Galilean. Corpses have a way of announcing their presence most forcefully. Especially in warm climates.

If they had the body—one of them, or two or three, or all of them together—if they had the body, how do we account for their heroic

---

If their testimony was not true, there was was no possible motive for its fabrication.[2]
—*Simon Greenleaf*

---

courage in the face of intense and increasing opposition? Did they risk their lives for a story they knew to be a lie?

Second Accusation: Someone Else Took the Body

Maybe someone else took it and did not tell the disciples. Maybe Joseph decided he wanted his tomb back, so he came and took the body out.

How did he get by the soldiers? And where did he put it?

Maybe the women did it. Maybe they took the body outside so they could finish their embalming in the daylight.

---

2. Quoted in Wilbur M. Smith, *Therefore Stand* (Nantick, Mass., W. A. Wilde Company, 1945), p. 425.

Then why didn't they put it back? Surely they couldn't afford a better tomb. And then there were the soldiers.

Or maybe someone else took it.

Did the soldiers? Did Pilate? Did one of the chief priests? Or several of them working together? Or several Pharisees?

Do you think Jesus' enemies would have remained silent when Peter stood before a festival crowd and said Jesus was alive? Do you think they would have resorted to threats and beatings and prison and murder, trying to contain this spreading new faith, when all they had to do was produce the dead body of Jesus?

They did not produce the dead body because they could not! How His enemies wished they knew where the body was! Yet never one time did any of Jesus' attackers deny that His tomb was empty. At no time did a single voice say, "We know where the body is."

Jesus' body was not in Joseph's grave or any other grave. Jesus' body was alive again. He was working with His disciples, actively preparing them for the time when He would return to the Father and they would carry on His work.

Where Was the Body?

Whoever took the body out of the tomb surely wasn't in much of a hurry. First they removed the head covering and folded it. Then they found a way to take the body but leave the burial cloth still lying where it was.

All this after they had shoved the door out of the way, of course. Ever try pushing a stone door?

Now all they needed to do was carry the body—if you've ever lifted someone who was unconscious or dead you know what that's like—and get away without being seen by the guards.

Once that was done, all they had to do was find a place to hide it. Yes, and keep absolutely silent when the apostles began telling everywhere that Jesus was alive again.

Do you believe that is what happened?

Accusation: The Women Went to the Wrong Tomb

If no one has the body, maybe it is still there some place. Maybe Mary went to the wrong tomb. Maybe when she didn't find Jesus' body, she ran to the disciples with the tale, "Jesus is alive." Maybe Jesus' tomb was too difficult to find.

If that's true, then it must have been hard to find Golgotha too, because we know from someone who was there that the tomb was very close to the place Jesus was crucified (John 19:41,42). Besides, Mary had watched the burial (Mark 15:47). Can we believe she couldn't find the place again?

The tomb belonged to Joseph of Arimathea (Matthew 27:57-60). He claimed the body, and he and Nicodemus did the actual burying (Jonn 19:38-42). Several women among Jesus' followers watched to see where He was buried, then went home and prepared spices and perfumes to use after the Sabbath was over. They took note of the place because they expected to come back. Do you think none of them remembered?

Do you think Joseph would forget where his own tomb was? Or Nicodemus, would he forget how to get back to the place he had helped bury Jesus?

That tomb was chiseled out of rock in a rich man's garden close to execution hill. They weren't trying to locate one of a dozen graves dug in flat ground.

Several years ago an unbeliever suggested that the women were crying so much that in their grief and tears they missed the right place, and a young man saw them and tried to tell they they were wrong: "He's not here; he is over there." Startled, the women ran off, hearing only the first part of the boy's message. Then they allowed their imaginations to go to work and told the disciples Jesus had been raised from the dead.

Is that what you think happened?

If you were Joseph of Arimathea and someone told you that a body you had put in your own cemetery had come back to life, what would you do? Don't you think you might go down and check it out?

Is Nicodemus going to sit still while Jerusalem is ablaze with talk of Jesus' resurrection? No, he is going to go and see whether that body is still where he and Joseph put it. And if it is, do you think he is going to keep silent?

Accusation: Jesus Wasn't Really Dead

Every now and then someone offers the possibility that Jesus had carefully planned His "death" and "resurrection." For example, one theory suggests that as He cried "I thirst," a confederate slipped Him a powerful drug that induced unconsciousness, signalling His disciples to run to Pilate for permission to take Him down. This done, Jesus spent the next couple of days recuperating, and on Sunday "rose again."

They overlook all that happened before and during Jesus' crucifixion.

Scourging was a terrible punishment. Jewish law forbade more than forty lashes, but the Romans showed no mercy. Victims sometimes died under the whip.

His back raw, His scalp and forehead lacerated, bruises on His body, Jesus was stretched across two rough-hewn timbers while nails were pounded through His hands and feet. Thus fastened, He was raised aloft to hang in increasing pain and exhaustion.

When His body finally sagged unmoving, His followers thought He died. The soldiers thought He died. The centurion, charged with putting the prisoners to death, thought He died. Taking no chances, he speared the body to be sure. He would forfeit his life if he were mistaken.

John, standing close enough to see it all, thought Jesus was dead. The priests thought Jesus was dead. Pilate thought Jesus was dead. The guards posted at the tomb thought He was dead.

Putting on an act? Some kind of drug or faint? Every person there would scoff at the idea.

So would those who saw Jesus after His resurrection. A person who had experienced what Jesus went through would need sympa-

---

If those who don't believe have to keep inventing new theories to explain away the resurrection, doesn't that in itself tell us something significant?

---

thy and care three days later, yet Mary Magdalene offers none. Instead, she falls at His feet in worship.

The women, suddenly meeting Jesus, do the same.

The two travelers on their way to Emmaus don't suspect that their companion has been tied to a post and brutally whipped three days before; worse, that He has been nailed to a cross. Weren't they walking? And wasn't it seven miles?

When Jesus, that same evening, displays His wounds to the disciples, they don't see swollen flesh, tender and painful. The marks are there, but those hands and feet will never hurt again.

Jesus doesn't talk like someone fighting fever and loss of blood. With assurance and power He points them to the waiting world, and tells how they will go everywhere in His name.

Didn't really die? That accusation simply doesn't fit.

Accusation: The Disciples Only Thought
They Were Seeing Jesus

The priests and Pharisees were malicious in their accusation that the disciples stole the body. Others try to be more kind, saying, "No, we aren't accusing the disciples of lying. It is just that they were mistaken. They thought they were seeing Jesus."

They thought they were seeing a ghost. Jesus showed them His hands and feet and talked with them, but that wasn't enough. Then He asked if they had anything to eat (Luke 24:36-43). They were not easy to convince.

Nor was Thomas. He demanded proof. Jesus gladly submitted to the very test Thomas proposed. If Thomas' doubts went beyond the others', so did His response. When Jesus showed His hands and side, Thomas cried out, "My Lord and my God!" (John 20:24-28). He could not possibly doubt any longer.

Is the resurrection of Jesus only hallucination? Did the disciples manufacture the risen Christ out of their own shattered hopes? Look at it again. Where is the evidence that a single one of them expected Him to come back? They were crushed, their dreams broken.

When reports started coming that Jesus was alive again, they didn't believe them. "Their words seemed to them like nonsense" (Luke 24:11). Thomas refused to believe his fellow apostles! On the mountain in Galilee as Jesus was preparing to issue the Great Commission, some in that crowd still doubted (Matthew 28:17).

We hear from those who deny that Jesus' body came from the grave that it was only a "spiritual" resurrection. That may be one-half inch removed from the "vision" theory, but it is equally false.

If Jesus' body still lies in Palestine, He runs a poor third behind Enoch and Elijah, who were spared death. Perhaps we ought to look to one of them for hope in a life to come. Not even an unbeliever would suggest that!

Accusation: The Records Are Not Reliable

Handling our leather-bound New Testaments, with their pages edged in gold, we sometimes forget that here are firsthand records published during the lifetime of some of the principals.

Matthew was one of the Twelve. Mark was closely associated with Simon Peter (Acts 12:1-17; 1 Peter 5:13). Luke "carefully investigated everything from the beginning" (Luke 1:3). John personally examined the empty tomb and talked many times with Jesus after the resurrection (John 20:3—21:25).

To accept Christ's Resurrection is to have in our hearts the key to the Incarnation, it is to know the reason for the phenomenal power and growth of the early church, it is to have peace in our souls, because we are justified before God, and it is to know a joy that nothing can ever take away from us, because our hope is not in the circumstances of the things about us, but in the risen Saviour, confident that we have an inheritance incorruptible and undefiled, reserved in heaven for us, who are being kept here on earth by the same power of God that raised our Lord from the dead.[3]

Scholars have documented passages from New Testament books quoted in other writings of that era and trace the records back to the very days of the apostles.[4] Paul speaks of over five hundred witnesses to the resurrection, most of them still living at the time he wrote (1 Corinthians 15:6).

We are not looking at a fable made up long afterward and circulated among gullible illiterates.

Accusation: The Records Are Full of Contradictions

Three years ago I had an automobile accident. I had pulled out onto an icy street, was exceeding the twenty-five mile speed limit. I saw a trailer-truck hauling coal coming toward me, which I thought I recognized. I glanced up to see who was driving, and suddenly a big crew-cab pulled out from behind the truck and blocked the road.

When the lady driving the crew-cab saw me, she froze. By that time I had hit the brakes and was sliding toward her. She screamed, the older woman on the passenger side was yelling, and in slow motion I went right into her truck.

---

3. Wilbur M. Smith, *Therefore Stand* (Nantick, Mass., W.A. Wilde Company, 1945), p. 437.

4. See J.W. McGarvey, *Evidences of Christianity* (Cincinnati, The Standard Publishing Company, 1886), and others.

The apologetics section of your Christian bookstore will have other sources of help in studying the resurrection. These are representative of the many books available:

Josh McDowell, *Evidence That Demands a Verdict* (Here's Life Publishers, Inc., San Bernadino, CA, 1972, 78).

William Lane Craig, *The Son Rises* (Chicago, Moody Press, 1981).

Paul E. Little, *KnowWhy You Believe* (Wheaton, Victor Books, 1967, 82).

Her husband came running out of the house, and I got out and went across the street to call the Highway Patrol.

In court she testified that she remembered no truck passing her house, but she thought I was driving too fast. Her husband did not see the truck, and neither did her son, who was in the front yard. However, another eyewitness testified that there was a truck. I had the driver's name, but he was not called to testify, as he did not see the crash. My testimony was different from that of the other driver, and other eyewitnesses also gave different testimony. Does that imply that there never was a collision between my car and her crew-cab?

The judge didn't think so. Taking all the evidence into consideration, he was able to reconstruct the total picture, assigning eighty percent of the responsibility to her and twenty percent to me.

Matthew gives us information not found in John, and Luke tells us about things we don't get from the others. Does that mean there was no resurrection? Does it mean the records are not accurate in what they do tell?

What do you think?

It is by combining the data given by all of these four independent witnesses that we complete our understanding of what took place.

John Fitzgerald Kennedy, thirty-fifth President of the United States, died when struck in the head by a shot from a 6.5 Mannlicher-Carcano rifle. He was attended by Dr. Malcolm Perry, Surgeon Charles James, and others. Attempts at resuscitation failed, and Kennedy lies buried at Arlington National Cemetery, Washington, D. C.

Jesus of Nazareth died on a cross during a Jewish feast, in the presence of the disciple John, His mother Mary, and others. Three days later they saw Him alive again.

Kennedy and Jesus both died in real places, were seen and cared for by real people. Both were buried in real cemeteries. But there the similarity ends.

Kennedy still lies at Arlington.

And where do you think Jesus is?

Think It Over

Have a friend make a list of reasons not to believe that Jesus rose from the dead. You make a list of reasons to believe that He did. Compare your lists and talk about your reasons.

Now that he was not afraid to die, he was not afraid to live, either.

If You Knew You Would Live Forever

In his early sixties and in perfect health, Jack went to the doctor for his annual physical. "The doctor said I'd live to be a hundred," he said laughingly to a friend. That was Tuesday. Not that Wednesday but the next he had a stroke, and died before dawn on Thursday. "Live to be a hundred"?

The scene: A sixth-floor room in a large Midwestern hospital. The patient, a woman, is propped up in bed, listening intently to the man dressed in hospital greens standing next to her. The patient's family crowd into the little room, her husband in the chair by the foot of her bed, one son over by the window, another son and the daughter-in-law to his left.

The doctor, a neurosurgeon, explains his diagnosis.

"It is a tumor," he told them, "in this area." He placed his hand on the back of his head just above and behind his right ear. His audience listened in shocked silence.

The doctor talked slowly, giving patient and family time to assimilate what he was saying.

"I would estimate it to be the size of a lemon. It's been there for a long time, possibly twenty years, growing slowly and doubling in size about every year. That doesn't mean much when it is only one cell or a cluster of cells, but now we can't have it grow any larger than it is.

"I am ninety-five percent certain it is benign, but it has to come out. It will only continue to grow and cause more problems."

The ashen figure in the bed was the one who put their anxiety into words: "Am I going to live?"

We always want to know, don't we: "How long do I have?" In the case of the patient in Room 628, the answer was, "The chances are, I would say, fifty-fifty."

Fortunately, she came through her surgery, had no complications or paralysis, and is today living a normal life.

What if we could live forever? There is a group who are given a one hundred percent chance—much better than her doctor's estimate of fifty-fifty—and we're not talking about some remote tribe in the Asian highlands who eat boiled rope and sleep standing on their heads.

Who are these fortunates? Jesus' disciples! When He told them, "Because I live, you also will live" (John 14:19), He wasn't kidding.

At First, Disciples Were Afraid

How did the disciples react when Jesus laid this word on them? Was all their fear of death banished by that assurance of life? Before the night was over we find the disciples running off in all directions, trying to get as far away from Jesus as they can. Check it out in Matthew 26:56.

Don't stop there. Let's keep going.

> Those who had arrested Jesus took him to Caiaphas, the high priest, where the teachers of the law and the elders had assembled. But Peter followed him at a distance.
>
> —Matthew 26:57, 58

At a distance! At a distance? Wasn't Peter the one who promised that he would die before disowning Christ? Look at Matthew 26:35.

But things get worse. Peter and John have gone into the high priest's courtyard, and Peter is standing with several of the servants and officials around a fire trying to keep warm. First a servant girl, then another, then someone else, asks if he is a follower of Jesus. Each time Peter denies it; each time more emphatically.

What are you afraid of, Peter?

Are you afraid of ridicule?

Are you afraid of pain? Afraid they'll beat you or hit you?

Is it prison, Peter? Are you afraid you'll go to jail?

Or is it death? The ultimate fear. The basic fear. After all, Jesus is on trial for His life. Are you afraid of dying, Peter?

Let's leave Simon Peter and look at someone else for a moment. In the first verse of Acts 8 we meet a man who will become one of the most influential men in history. Our introduction to Saul of Tarsus horrifies us—he's giving approval to the mob action that stones Stephen to death.

Nor is that the end. From this murder scene Saul embarks on a campaign to destroy the church, going from house to house and dragging off every Christian he can find to prison (Acts 8:3).

Saul cannot stand this new faith. He believes Jesus is an imposter and His followers are renegades. Saul sets out for Damascus, intent on stamping out Christianity and everyone connected with it.

> As he neared Damascus on his journey, suddenly a light from heaven flashed around him. He fell to the ground and heard a voice say to him, "Saul, Saul, why do you persecute me?"
>
> "Who are you, Lord?" Saul asked.
>
> "I am Jesus, whom you are persecuting," he replied. "Now get up and go into the city, and you will be told what you must do."
>
> —Acts 9:3-6

Saul met Jesus. Saul had thought Jesus was dead, but here was Jesus alive again and talking to him!

Saul was never the same after that. He was baptized, and now tried to bring people to the very faith he had tried to destroy. In time he even changed his name. Saul the persecutor became Paul the Christian preacher.

Look at how his life changed.

He had been a respected Pharisee, a scholar trained by the great teacher Gamaliel, comfortable and secure in his well-ordered world. Now, as a Christian, Paul lost all that, except the training, and he had to rethink that drastically.

He was driven out of Pisidian Antioch, expelled by the civic leaders (Acts 13:50, 51). He was threatened in Iconium (Acts 14:5), brutally stoned and nearly killed at Lystra (Acts 14:19).

How did Paul take this? Did he stop preaching? Did his critics silence him? Hardly. Look at the record. Everyone thought he was dead after being stoned at Lystra, but Paul got up and went back into the city, then he and Barnabas left for Derbe. Did they quit? Were they going back home? Just the opposite.

> They preached the good news in that city and won a large number of disciples. Then they returned to Lystra, Iconium, and Antioch, strengthening the disciples and encouraging them to remain true to the faith. "We must go through many hardships to enter the kingdom of God," they said.
> —Acts 14:21, 22

Despite arrest, ridicule, constant danger, and incessant persecution, Paul continued to tell everyone he met about Jesus Christ. Paul describes his experiences in a letter to his friends at Corinth:

> Five times I received from the Jews the forty lashes minus one. Three times I was beaten with rods, once I was stoned, three times I was shipwrecked, I spent a night and a day in the open sea, I have been constantly on the move. I have been in danger from rivers, in danger from bandits, in danger from my own countrymen, in danger from Gentiles; in danger in the city, in danger in the country, in danger at sea; and in danger from false brothers. I have labored and toiled and have often gone without sleep; I have known hunger and thirst and have often gone without food; I have been cold and naked. Besides everything else, I face daily the pressure of my concern for all the churches.
> —2 Corinthians 11:24-28

Fear Changed to Courage

Why the change from persecutor to preacher, from militant unbeliever to enthusiastic Christian? Read Paul's own explanation, given earlier in that same letter:

> For Christ's love compels us, because we are convinced that one died for all, and therefore all died. And he died for all, that those who live should no longer live for themselves but for him who died for them and was raised again.
> —2 Corinthians 5:14, 15

From the time he had become a Christian, Paul was never again afraid to die. Jesus Christ had overcome death! Now that he was not afraid to die, Paul was not afraid to live, either. He wrote this to the churches in Galatia:

I have been crucified with Christ and I no longer live, but Christ lives in me. The life I live in the body, I live by faith in the Son of God, who loved me and gave himself for me.
—Galatians 2:20

Without being neurotic or suicidal, Paul could actually look forward to dying, knowing he would go to be with Christ (Philippians 1:21-24). Paul's life goal had changed from looking out for himself to looking forward to Heaven.

I want to know Christ and the power of his resurrection and the fellowship of sharing in his sufferings, becoming like him in his death, and so, somehow, to attain to the resurrection from the dead.
—Philippians 3:10, 11

We see a similar change from fear to courage in Peter. During Jesus' trial Peter was so afraid that he let a servant girl wring from him a denial that he even knew Christ. Yet less than two months later Peter stood in the same city before a crowd composed

---

*The Christian gospel affirms that
death is serious but not fatal.*
—Dr. James D. Strauss

---

in part of the very people responsible for Jesus' death, and he fearlessly exposed their guilt: "You, with the help of wicked men, put him to death by nailing him to the cross" (Acts 2:23). But Peter didn't stop there. He went on:

But God raised him from the dead, freeing him from the agony of death, because it was impossible for death to keep its hold on him.... God has raised this Jesus to life, and we are all witnesses of the fact.... Therefore let all Israel be assured of this: God has made this Jesus, whom you crucified, both Lord and Christ.
—Acts 2:24-36

Was that servant girl in the crowd? Did she hear Peter, who had denied Jesus, now speaking so boldly? That man who had challenged Peter at the high priest's house (John 18:26, 27)—did he now wonder what had changed this disciple?

Peter's announcement met with acceptance as three thousand were baptized into Christ. Opposition surfaced almost at once, however.

One afternoon he and John were going into the temple. They met a crippled man and Peter healed him. Immediately a crowd gathered, and Peter used his opportunity to preach.

Quickly the authorities arrested Peter and John and put them into jail. Their crime: "Because the apostles were teaching the people and proclaiming in Jesus the resurrection of the dead" (Acts 4:2).

How did imprisonment affect Peter? Brought out the next day for questioning, Peter didn't hesitate:

> Rulers and elders of the people! If we are being called to account today for an act of kindness shown to a cripple and are asked how he was healed, then know this, you and everyone else in Israel: It is by the name of Jesus Christ of Nazareth, whom you crucified but whom God raised from the dead, that this man stands before you completely healed.
>
> —Acts 4:8-10

When they were released, Peter and John went back to the church and told what had happened. Instead of being intimidated, the group asked God for boldness! Forcefully and effectively "the apostles continued to testify to the resurrection of the Lord Jesus" (Acts 4:33).

Summoned to court again, they were ordered to stop their teaching. Their reaction?

> Peter and the other apostles replied: "We must obey God rather than men! The God of our fathers raised Jesus from the dead.... We are witnesses of these things."
>
> —Acts 5:29-32

No empty threats this time; the authorities had the apostles beaten, then ordered them never to speak in the name of Jesus.

Were the apostles silenced? They rejoiced "because they had been counted worthy of suffering disgrace for the Name" (Acts

5:41). Day after day, in public and in private, they kept telling others about Christ, and the heart of that message was His resurrection!

Even after Saul's persecution began, Peter continued. To the Gentile, Cornelius, he said, "They killed him by hanging him on a tree, but God raised him from the dead" (Acts 10:39, 40); in his letters Peter writes of Jesus' resurrection and the assurance it gives us:

> Praise be to the God and Father of our Lord Jesus Christ! In his great mercy he has given us new birth into a living hope through the resurrection of Jesus Christ from the dead, and into an inheritance that can never perish, spoil or fade—kept in heaven for you.
>
> —1 Peter 1:3, 4

That great challenge to Christian living with which Peter closes his second letter would be utter nonsense—even mockery—without the resurrection. Peter had no uncertainties here. He had seen Jesus alive again. Peter was so certain that he was going to live forever as Jesus had promised that he could write of his approaching death calmly and without fear (2 Peter 1:13, 14).

Christ's Resurrection Was Central to the Early Church

Take Jesus' resurrection from the preaching of the early church and you have nothing left. At Paphos, on his first missionary tour, Paul briefly sketched God's dealings through history and then led into Jesus' coming. Here's part of Paul's message:

> Though they found no proper ground for a death sentence, they asked Pilate to have him executed. When they had carried out all that was written about him, they took him down from the tree and laid him in a tomb. But God raised him from the dead, and for many days he was seen by those who had traveled with him from Galilee to Jerusalem. They are now his witnesses to our people.
>
> —Acts 13:28-31

Whether in the synagogue in Thessalonica (Acts 17:3), or to the philosophers in Athens (Acts 17:18, 31); before the Sanhedrin (Acts 23:6) or King Agrippa (Acts 26:23), Paul stressed the resurrection of Jesus Christ.

What was it that filled the early church with such joy and power? It was their assurance that Jesus had achieved victory over death and that they would share in this triumph. Paul links Jesus' resurrection and our forgiveness in Acts 13:37-39, and both Paul and Peter join baptism and the resurrection, seeing baptism as a picture of

---

Before, I was so scared I would cry at night because I didn't understand so many things. But now as I learn more I feel less frightened.

—Ohio Student

Jesus' death, burial, and resurrection and of our own death to sin, burial with Christ, and resurrection to a new life (Romans 6:1-14; 1 Peter 3:18-21).

We've heard it so often that we're no longer moved—hardly even nudged—by this unparalleled series of events: Jesus of Nazareth was lashed until His back was raw, was nailed to a wooden cross, hung there until He died in agony, while His enemies laughed in His face. The bloody remains were buried, and the tomb was sealed and guarded. Three days later He came back to life. After several weeks with His disciples and commissioning them to tell the world, He went back to Heaven, promising to come again.

This was the message that captured the Mediterranean world, that enabled Christians to accept and endure misunderstanding, persecution, and death. By this they lived; by this message they died, confident they would live again.

Opposition to Teaching About the Resurrection

She was young and in love and wanted to marry the handsome young man she'd met in college. From the way he looked at her, the counselor could see that the young man was in love, too. They made a striking couple, his swarthy complexion contrasting with her fair skin and blue eyes.

Slight problem: he was from the Middle East and was a Moslem; she was from America and was a Christian.

"I am Moslem only in my birth," the young man explained to the counselor. "We in my family are not going as you Christians are going to your meetings and we do not study the book."

The counselor nodded. "Yes, we have some of our people who do not go to our meetings, also. May I ask you about Jesus Christ? Do you know about Him?"

"I know of Him, yes," came the answer. "He is a messenger from God. God sends messengers: Moses, Jesus, Mohammed; they are the same."

"Do you know of Jesus' resurrection?"

"He came back?" The young man grinned. "He didn't come back to life. You say he came back?" The boy grinned again and nearly laughed aloud until he saw the look on his girl friend's face.

Festus almost laughed at Paul, too, upon hearing of Jesus' resurrection: "You are out of your mind, Paul!" he shouted. "Your great learning is driving you insane" (Acts 26:24).

Paul flatly denied that he was insane (Acts 26:25). What he taught was true and reasonable. If some thought it was foolish (1 Corinthians 1:23), he was willing to be called a fool for the sake of Christ (1 Corinthians 4:10). Since the Master himself was despised and rejected, His followers should not be surprised if they were scorned when they proclaimed His resurrection. And indeed they were scorned in many places.

Some of the Athenians sneered (Acts 17:32). The Sanhedrin erupted in a near-riot over this question, and troops were sent in to rescue Paul and keep him from being torn to pieces (Acts 23:6-10).

Yet the early Christians kept up their testimony. Peter was not the only one who declared, "We cannot help speaking about what we have seen and heard" (Acts 4:20).

For Further Research

1. How did the early church know for sure that Jesus had come back from the dead? See Acts 2:32; 3:15; 4:20; 5:32; 10:41; and 13:31.

2. How do we, today, know for sure that Jesus rose?

3. Were there many who saw Jesus after He had come back from the dead? See 1 Corinthians 15:1-8.

Not one person—not one!—of those who saw Jesus after He had come back to life ever changed his mind and said he was mistaken. The early Christians changed their minds on other things—about opening the doors to the Gentiles, about where to preach, about whether or not Christians should observe the old dietary laws—but to their deaths they kept telling how Jesus had come back from the dead and was alive now.

The Difference It Makes

When you're sure you are going to live forever, you tend to see things differently. Possessions, for example. You realize that possessions are only temporary. They become outdated, need replacing.

Do you have any of these at your house: washboard? churn? carpet beater? icepick? asafetida bag? Your great-grandmother knew what they were and probably used them all. She might not know what to do with some of your things: thermostat, microwave, video game, moped, weed whip.

Knowing you're going to live forever helps you see that we are always users, never owners, of possessions. Measuring them against eternity helps keep things in proper perspective.

We see life differently when we know we're going to live forever. We are freed from the aimless drifting that hinders so many. Knowing that our goal is Heaven, we live by a higher standard. We have stronger motivation in our struggle against the world's slow corrosion.

We look at death differently, too. The grim reaper loses some of its terror in the light of Jesus' promises. With Paul we may sing, "Where, O death, is your victory? Where, O death, is your sting?" (1 Corinthians 15:55). To be with Jesus is "better by far" than to stay here (Philippians 1:23), though we remain here cheerfully till He calls us home.

We even see Jesus differently when we know we're going to live forever. Some see Him as a super safety net, there in case of trouble, but most of the time taken for granted. Some see Him as an "extra," important but sort of like dessert. "I need something to eat, a place to live, an education, transportation, and oh, yes, I'll be a Christian, too."

When we realize that only Jesus opens the door to forever, we see Him differently. Not an extra, or an unwanted interruption, He becomes the very center of life in this world and the next.

A young preacher was calling on an older woman who was in the last stages of cancer. Not quite knowing what to say, the young minister talked in general terms about the church, then rose to leave. But he lingered for a moment, fearing, as many of us do in such a situation, that he was not being helpful.

"Can I do anything for you?" he offered.

"Are you asking if I am afraid to die?" she answered softly. "I am not afraid to die. I know the Lord, and I am not afraid."

She knew that she would live forever.

Think It Over

1. You can trace the course of the disciples' feelings from unbelief and fear to belief and courage. Look up these references in Luke's Gospel. Which ones show unbelief? Which show the change to belief? Who are the individuals in each case?

- Luke 24:4 "wondering"
- Luke 24:5 "fright"
- Luke 24:8 "then they remembered his words"
- Luke 24:9 "they told all these things to the Eleven"
- Luke 24:11 "but they did not believe the women, because their words seemed to them like nonsense"
- Luke 24:12 "he went away, wondering to himself"
- Luke 24:31 "they recognized him"
- Luke 24:37 "they were startled and frightened, thinking they saw a ghost"
- Luke 24:41 "they still did not believe it because of joy and amazement"
- Luke 24:52 "they worshiped him."

2. Matthew, Mark, and John saw this same change. Check into each of those Gospels and trace what happened.

If your beliefs are no different from those of the world, why should your life be?

What If There Is No Resurrection From the Dead?

Have you ever asked yourself, "What if?"
"What if I were taller?"
"What if I were smarter?"
"What if I had more money?"
"What if I had blonde hair?"
"What if I were the boss?"
"What if I asked You Know Who to go out with me? And what if You Know Who said Yes?"

All fiction is a "What if." Herman Melville asked himself: "What if a half-crazy sea captain became obsessed with a certain enormous white whale?" He wrote what has been called the Great American Novel.

The only serious contender for the G.A.N. title was another "What if," this one by a southern belle who asked, "What if I would set a boy-meets-girl in Atlanta during the Civil War?" On movie screens across the country Clark Gable and Vivien Leigh still relive Margaret Mitchell's epic.[1]

Paul offered a "What if" in his first letter to the church at Corinth, and it is one we'd better take a look at. You wouldn't want to be waiting for a future that's not coming, or to cancel one that is.

---

1. Melville's book was *Moby Dick;* Margaret Mitchell's was *Gone With the Wind*

Corinth was a large commercial city built on a natural crossroads in Southern Greece. North/south and east/west highways ran through Corinth, and traders and builders and craftsmen—and homosexuals and thieves and prostitutes[2]—took advantage of the people and money flowing through the city. Naturally such a place was more noted for commerce and prosperity and pleasure than for uprightness and morality. Drawing their wealth from seaborne trade, the pagan Corinthians praised Poseidon, the sea god; but Corinthians and visitors gave more ardent devotion to Aphrodite, goddess of love. In her famous temple a thousand dedicated prostitutes waited to serve the worshipers who brought liberal offerings.

The Jews of Corinth had nothing to do with the pagan gods or the prevailing immorality, but Paul's experiences had shown that pious Jews were often hostile towards Christianity.

Corinth would not seem like a very good place to start a church, but Paul came here on his second missionary journey and began working. Before long, despite violent opposition, he won many people to Christ.[3] Rather than go on a new field as he usually did, Paul stayed for a while, and the church grew.

After Paul left, changes crept in. Some of the people were even denying the resurrection.

If they had come to Christ from a Jewish background, they may have been influenced by the Sadducees, who said there was no resurrection (Matthew 22:23). Those coming from paganism had grown up with the Greek concept that the body was the prison house of the soul, and that death released the soul from captivity. To people who thought like that, a resurrection of the body was not a blessing, but a calamity.[4]

Maybe there were other objections, much like some we hear today: "What about someone who dies after a lingering illness? You surely don't expect him to carry around that wasted body forever, do you?" Or, "I know of someone who was in an accident. Will he still be maimed after the resurrection?"

Let's look at how Paul answers.

2. 1 Corinthians 6:9-11

3. Acts 18:6-8

4. J. W. McGarvey and Philip Y. Pendleton, *The Standard Bible Commentary: Thessalonians, Corinthians, Galatians, and Romans* (Cincinnati: The Standard Publishing Company Co., 1916), P. 145

"May I Remind You of What I Preached and What You Believed"

1 Corinthians 15:1-11

The unchanging heart of the gospel is that God came to earth in the person of His Son, sacrificed himself for our sins, was buried in a tomb that was sealed and guarded, and then was raised to life on the third morning, never to die again—and that He freely shares His victory with anyone who will accept it.

It was no easier then to win people to Christ than it is now, and Paul reminds them that never once had he resorted to gimmicks or high pressure to bring people into the church. Christ had been central from the very first (1 Corinthians 2:1-5), and His resurrection was *always* an integral part of the gospel.

Removed as we are by time and distance, we may forget that anyone in Corinth who wanted to could board one of the ships in the harbor at Cenchrea, less than four miles away, could sail down the Aegean and across the Mediterranean to Caesarea or Joppa, could go up to Jerusalem, could walk around on Golgotha, could enter and examine the empty tomb, could find eyewitnesses to Jesus' trial and crucifixion, could talk to people who had seen and talked with Him after the resurrection, several of whom had heard His last words and watched as He ascended to the Father. Paul was talking about facts—facts that were verifiable, provable. More than five hundred people had seen Jesus after He rose, and most of these people were still alive (1 Corinthians 15:6).

Paul's own experience had to be reckoned with by anyone who tried to deny the resurrection. Hadn't he been one of the worst persecutors of the church? Hadn't he been known for his disbelief in Christ and his determination to stamp out His followers?

What convinced Paul was not theological debate; it was the sight of the living Jesus confronting him on the highway near Damascus. It was Jesus' words; it was the conversation. It was the undeniable fact that the very one Paul had thought was a fraud was not dead but was very much alive. Paul could never forget that, and he reminded his friends at Corinth of how it had affected him.

How could they have forgotten it? They had surely heard him tell about it before. What were they thinking, anyway? Why were they so unsure now of the fact of which they once had been so sure?

Didn't they remember the prophecies of Isaiah and David and Daniel and others? Were the Corinthians forgetting those predictions of Jesus' death *and resurrection?*

If There Is No Resurrection, Then. . . ?

1 Corinthians 15:12-19

"How can you say there is no resurrection," Paul says, "after all the preaching about it?"

Suppose someone were to say, "Neil Armstrong walk on the moon? I don't believe it!" How could anyone deny that it happened when so many people have talked about it?

Before anyone could deny the resurrection, Paul challenged him to explain why so many had reported it. Why would anyone say that Jesus was alive again if He were not? What could they gain by spreading such falsehood?

And it was apparent that messengers had gone everywhere telling the news that Jesus was alive again, and like those talking about

---

I don't like the idea of being left out
night after night in a cold church-yard.
—Herman Melville[5]

Armstrong's moon walk, these were contemporaries to the event, many who were not sure it could be done but who were convinced by evidence that could not be denied.

Someone may say, "Suppose the critics are right and there is no resurrection. Does it really matter that much?"

Don't answer that until you look at the implications Paul lays out for his friends at Corinth in order for them to decide whether or not it matters.

Before we go much farther maybe we ought to be sure of one thing: dead people don't come back by themselves. There's nothing in human flesh or mind or spirit that can restore life. Paul consistently links *resurrection* and *God*.

It was God who raised Christ from the dead (1 Corinthians 15:15). To some who are in error regarding the resurrection, Paul directs the accusation that they are "ignorant of God" (1 Corinthians 15:34). Concerning what kind of body we will have, Paul cites the example of a seed: "God gives it a body as He had determined" (1 Corinthians 15:38), showing that God will provide the proper body in the resurrection, even as He provides resurrection itself.

---

5. In a letter to Samuel Savage, December 10, 1862

Satan brought death into the world. Life, including resurrection life, comes only from God.

Another thing we ought to look at is this: Paul is talking about life again after death. He is not talking about reincarnation; he is not talking about immortality in the memory of one's friends; he is not talking about a vague merging into some vast spirit-force in the hereafter. Paul is talking about being individually and personally raised to renewed life after death has ended this one.

There were some in the church at Corinth who said, "This cannot be. Dead people don't come back to life. You talk of a resurrection? Paul, there isn't any. It's impossible."

To them Paul says, "If there is no resurrection, then count Jesus out, too!"

Were the Corinthians looking at Jesus' resurrection and ours as being in some way different? Were they saying in effect, "Yes, Jesus did come back in His body, but that was so His disciples could recognize Him and know for sure there is life after death; however, for us it will be a 'spiritual' resurrection"?

Paul is emphatic: If we won't be raised from the dead, then Jesus wasn't either.

Part of Christ's purpose in coming was to identify with us, to become one with us that we might become one with Him. Is this identification to be severed at death, so that we only have some vague ethereal afterlife, while He was raised to live again in a recognizable body? Paul doesn't think so.

He goes on. "If Christ has not been raised, our preaching is useless and so is your faith" (1 Corinthians 15:14).

Suppose God had abandoned Jesus to rot in the ground. What would that say concerning faith and trust and obedience? If a supposedly loving God were to permit Satan to crush the noblest and purest life ever known and do nothing about it, every voice in Heaven and on earth would cry out in protest, "What kind of a God are You?" Who would believe in such a God?

If God didn't raise Jesus, Jesus is only another martyr, not the founder of a new faith, but a tragic hero, defeated at the end, penniless, almost friendless, rather pitiful. After all, He lived and died in absolute confidence that God would ultimately vindicate Him.

If there is no resurrection, Paul continues, "We are then found to be false witnesses" (1 Corinthians 15:15). Are we liars? Paul challenges the Corinthians to look at his life. They know what kind of person he is. Does he seem like a liar?

Worse, what of them? For if Christ is still in His grave, they are still in their sins. If Jesus is dead, then sin remains triumphant and they can forget about forgiveness.

The Christian dead they have buried in hope of resurrection—if Christ is not raised, then these are only mouldering corpses. They may as well have stayed in paganism. If death ended everything for them, where was the difference they hoped to find in Christ?

"But Christ Has Indeed Been Raised"
1 Corinthians 15:20-34

Now Paul moves to the positive side, and clearly states his thesis: "Christ has indeed been raised from the dead" (1 Corinthians 15:20).

Centuries before, the law told how the first grain to ripen should be offered to the Lord (Leviticus 23:9-14). Paul sees Jesus' resurrection as a preview of more resurrections to come, just as the firstfruit offering was a picture of the coming harvest.

He contrasts Adam and Christ. Sin's infection by Satan through Adam brought death, so redemption's cleansing was introduced by God through Christ. Adam brought us death; Jesus brings us life.

People may ask, "If God is God, why doesn't He do something about the suffering and injustice in the world?"

He has done something! God is waging a campaign against every form of suffering, tears, pain, sin, and wrong. God will conquer! His enemies will be vanquished! Even death, the last enemy, will finally be overcome.

> ### For Further Research
> 1. Matthew 12:39-41 records that Jesus compared His experience with Jonah's. After reading Jonah 1 and 2, what similarities do you see?
>
> 2. Write your own definition of "resurrection." Compare yours with the dictionary.
>
> 3. A well-known song says, "You ask me how I know He lives? He lives within my heart." In 1 Corinthians 15, does Paul refer to feelings to support the idea of Jesus' resurrection? What kind of evidence does he cite?

There is nothing in the universe that can withstand the power displayed in raising Jesus from the dead.

Death and hell conspired against Him to kill Him and keep Him in the grave, but these forces of sin and darkness were powerless to hold Him there.

In London's Westminster Abbey stands an ancient throne used for generations for the coronation of the English monarchs. Set into the wall immediately behind the throne, where the candidate must see it as he or she takes his place, are these words from Revelation 11:15:

The kingdoms of this world are become the kingdoms of our Lord, and of his Christ; and he shall reign for ever and ever.

Then Paul asked, "If the dead are not raised at all, why are people baptized for them?" Some scholars think this refers to baptism by proxy for people who have died unbaptized, but the Bible has no other hint of such a practice. Other scholars see Paul's words in the light of his explanation of baptism in Romans 6:1-14, which shows that baptism links us to Jesus' dying for us, being buried, and being raised for us.

That link is plain, whatever may be the precise meaning of "baptized for the dead." In baptism we act out Jesus' death, burial, and resurrection; we picture our own death to sin and our rising to a new kind of life; and we give a preview of our coming physical death, burial, and resurrection. If there were no resurrection, baptism would lose much of its meaning.

If there were no resurrection, then Paul's way of life would not make sense. "Why," he asks, "do we endanger ourselves every hour?" (1 Corinthians 15:30). It would be foolish to risk his life to proclaim the gospel of salvation if there were no life after death.

In a letter written from a prison house Paul tells how he had given up everything to suffer hardship and persecution and trials. Then he tells why:

I want to know Christ and the power of his resurrection and the fellowship of sharing in his sufferings, becoming like him in his death, and so, somehow, to attain to the resurrection from the dead.

—Philippians 3:10, 11

If there were no resurrection, Paul would indeed be pitiable (1 Corinthians 15:19). So would all of us who trust in Jesus for eternal life. If there were nothing beyond the grave, then it would be just as well to eat and drink and have fun today, for tomorrow death would end all. Our work for the Lord would be wasted, our offerings would be thrown away, our suffering would be for nothing if there were no resurrection. If there were no resurrection, then life would be meaningless.

"What Kind of Body?"
1 Corinthians 15:35-49

"What kind of body are we going to have?" For some, that's the big question. Paul uses several illustrations to answer the question, but it can all be summed up in two statements: "Don't worry about that; let God take care of it."

You plant a seed in the ground. It decomposes and dies and becomes roots and stem and leaves. You couldn't dig for it and find it, but new life comes from that seed. When this body is buried it will decay and disappear. But as God brings new life from the seed, so He will bring new life to us.

Our form may be different—as the plant is from the seed—but each of us will still be the same person.

Look at the variety in God's creation. Why do we suppose the resurrection body has to be identical to this human frame? At birth God gave us a body adapted to the needs of this life; in the resurrection God will give us a body suited to our new life.

Of course we will be changed. How could we not be?

Here we are housed in decaying bodies of flesh. There we will be forever freed from death and decay. Here we are subject to illness,

---

On the cross, God made our sorrows His;
In the empty tomb, He made His joy ours forever.

---

disease, pain; there we will be whole forever. Here we are confined by weakness; there we will be filled with power. Here we are of the earth; there we will be of eternity.

Paul wants us to know that our new selves will be far greater than our old. The old is of the earth; the new will be of Heaven.

"The Trumpet Will Sound"
1 Corinthians 15:50-57

This body of blood and flesh, destined to weakness and dishonor and death, is not fit to dwell in God's eternal realm, so there must be a change. But how?

Paul gives us a glimpse.

101

In an instant—at the summons of God's trumpet call (1 Thessalonians 4:16)—those who have died and those of us still living will be transformed. That in us which is perishable will be made imperishable; that which is mortal will be made immortal; that which is corruptible will be made incorruptible.

Sin's power will be broken. Death's curse will be gone—not suspended for a time; not temporarily delayed, but gone forever. Death will be gone forever.

The grim shadow that has fallen across man's path since Adam will be lifted. We can laugh death in the face!

"Death! Listen, Death; can you hear me? Where's your sting now? Where's your victory now, Death? Where is it, Death?"

Can we begin to see the scope of the victory gained by Jesus Christ?

Liberated to a new life of power and freedom in this world, with eternity unfolding before us, can we begin to see the love and grace that gladly offer LIFE to all who will take Jesus Christ as Lord?

"Give Yourselves Fully to the Work"
1 Corinthians 15:58

Paul closes with a challenge: Keep working. Be faithful. Don't be disturbed by difficulties along the way. Give yourselves completely to the work of Christ, knowing that the day of resurrection will more than repay for all your suffering and labor here.

The young preacher dreaded making the call, for each time he had seen his friend, she had been worse than the time before. Her wasted hand was hot to his touch; her eyes closed against even the faint light coming through the drawn blinds.

She was alone in her fifth-floor room. No one said so audibly, but it was common knowledge that this end of the hall was for terminal patients. And she was terminal. Terminal.

Cancer had brought this once lovely woman to this frightening skeleton of dying flesh.

Finally it came time to go. "I want to pray," he said, and started to bow his head.

"Don't pray for me to live," she whispered. "Don't pray for me to live; I want to go. I'm ready. I want to go."

It was not the cancer that made her say that; it was Christ. This woman loved the Lord, and during the long night hours she had often been awake and in prayer. No medication eased her into this attitude of waiting; she wanted to go to be with her Lord.

Were Jesus not raised, could she say that? Were Jesus not raised, could the young preacher pray that? Less than a week later, her prayer was answered. She is whole now, in that place where sickness becomes health; where weakness becomes power; where death becomes life.

Think It Over

1. Can you add to this list?

Jesus resurrection was a victory of...
life over death
joy over sorrow
truth over falsehood
good over evil
love over hatred.

2. Do you know people today who don't believe in the resurrection? What would you say to them?

3. Has your study of 1 Corinthians 15 added to your ideas on the resurrection, or changed your thinking? If so, what has been the change?

It is not death I fear, but dying.
                    —Montaigne

When Someone You Love Is Dying

Though we had been sitting in the hospital waiting room for hours, we still were not prepared when the hallway doors suddenly parted and Dr. Irons and Dr. Cummings appeared. They didn't have to say a word; we knew. Behind their masks of professionalism lay bad news. Their eyes gave them away.

Wasn't it only weeks ago Mother had complained of pain in her side? Everything had gone so fast. Visits to the doctor, then to a specialist. Tests and more tests. Now this.

My dad, my brother Jim, my sister Sandy, and I waited. I don't remember which doctor spoke first. Very simply they told us that mother's condition was terminal. They would do everything possible, but mother would not get well.

"How long does she have?"

"I would say about two years."

How does a family cope with a verdict like that? What do you do when someone you love is dying?

When the Diagnosis Is Terminal

When the diagnosis is terminal, the family often learns before the patient does. Mother was still in the recovery room. We were the ones who received this shattering blow. She was anesthetized; we were not.

104

How were we going to handle this? It couldn't be true. No, it couldn't be true. Did we have to tell her? When? How?

Sometimes the patient already suspects. He has been feeling this burning tightness in his chest but kept it to himself. She noticed the lump months ago, but said nothing until she discovered another swelling in her throat.

More often the diagnosis comes as a surprise, and the shocked reaction is one of denial.

Dr. Elisabeth Kubler-Ross, in her book *On Death and Dying*,[1] suggests five "stages of dying" which many persons experience in the course of a terminal illness. Briefly they may be summarized as follows.

1. *Denial.* "No, not me." The patient feels it cannot be true. The diagnosis must be wrong. His or her test results were confused with someone else's. The doctors made a mistake.

Perhaps this stage is necessary because it helps cushion the impact of the awful news.

2. *Rage and anger.* "Why me?" The patient strikes out at God, at life, at fate, at family, at the doctor. "What did I do to bring on this?"

Christians are not exempt from anger, even against God. We should not try to stifle such expressions, for the patient may need to let out his feelings. Is the anger against God? "God can take it," Dr. Ross would answer.

3. *Bargaining.* "Yes, me, but...." The patient recognizes that he is very ill, but tries to bargain, even with God. "Give me two more years until my daughter graduates." Or, "If I recover, I'll go to church every Sunday and be a better person."

Sometimes the bargaining involves the medical team. "Help me get through this surgery and go home for Christmas at least," or "Make me well enough so we can go on our vacation."

4. *Depression.* "Yes, me." Now it sinks in that he will soon die, and the patient thinks about all the things he will never get to do, the wrong things he has done to family and friends and God, the failures he has committed. This can be a very difficult time for him and his loved ones.

The patient may communicate his depression to others, causing them to feel guilt, helplessness, and despair. Some patients crawl into a shell and refuse to talk or eat, to think about anything but their own predicament.

---

1. Elisabeth Kubler-Ross, *On Death and Dying* (New York: The Macmillan Company, 1969).

5. *Acceptance.* "My time is near, and I am ready." Now the patient can die peacefully. He has come to terms with his situation, has taken care of his unfinished business, and is willing to let go.

Families can go through these stages also.

When confronted with the news that someone we love is going to die, we cry out, "It can't be true." We rage at life, at fate, at God. "Why him? Why her? What did we do to deserve this?"

Lazarus' family blamed Christ's late arrival for Lazarus' death. Both sisters greeted Him with the accusation, "Lord, if you had been here, my brother would not have died" (John 11:3-6, 21, 32).

We bargain too, sometimes negatively. A girl in Steubenville, Ohio, told her minister, "If God lets Mother die, I'm never going to church again."

Watching our loved one weaken and lose weight, seeing the effect of surgery or massive drug therapy, we feel anger and grief and

---

The moment of death is brief; dying can take days, weeks, months, sometimes years.

---

depression. Finally we see that death is approaching and we give up our loved one to God.

These stages are not clearly defined, nor are they present in every case, but remembering them may enable us to see what is taking place during a terminal illness and death.

Helpful Steps to Be Taken

Several things can be done to make the best of the situation, even when the illness is life-threatening.

First, the patient and those closest to him deserve an accurate diagnosis presented in clear and understandable terms. Basal cell carcinoma is not melanoma, though both are cancers; acute myelo-monoblastic leukemia and chronic anemia are both related to the blood, but they are not the same disease.

Diabetes, multiple sclerosis, and muscular dystrophy will kill if unchecked, but proper treatment can extend normal life for many years.

If you do not understand the diagnosis, ask the doctor to explain what it means in terms you can understand.

Often a family presses for details, or will ask how long a patient will live. Sometimes these questions are difficult to answer.

For example, many factors influence how long a patient may live: the patient's response to drugs; how strictly he or she will maintain the prescribed regimen of diet, treatment, and rest; the attitude and support of those around the patient; and the patient's own determination or lack of it.

My mother was given two years.

We prayed; the church prayed. She rigidly adhered to a strict diet, took the medication prescribed, was careful about getting adequate rest, and lived six years instead of the two predicted.

Without becoming a nuisance or making the doctor feel threatened, you can ask what treatment will be given and what some of the expected outcomes are. Of course, doctors cannot always be exact at this point either.

Should the patient be told?

That depends, but perhaps not upon what you think. It does not depend upon your personal feelings. Often family members say, "We cannot tell her; it would destroy her," when what they mean is "We cannot tell her; it would destroy us."

Are you saying, "I cannot face telling her. I don't want to cry in

---

*We fear not death, but the
incompleteness in our lives.
—leukemia patient, dying at thirty-one*

---

front of her and I can't stand to see her cry."

Is this not a form of denial? Maybe if we don't talk about it, it will go away. Do we actually believe we will make the situation better through pretense?

"Yes," we announce, "I'd sure want to be told if I had something terminal"; but we're not so quick with the news when confronted by the real thing, whether the patient is "I" or "my" mother, father, brother, sister, sweetheart, or close friend.

There are ways *not* to tell the patient: "Hey Kevin, they tell me you've got Hodgkins. That stuff will kill you, won't it?"

What can be worse than having a terminal illness? It may be worse to learn that everybody else knows you have it, and that even those you trusted the most are part of the conspiracy of deception.

An important guideline for now and throughout the course of the illness is this: Let the patient lead.

When he asks, "What did the doctor say?" tell him, in words that are both honest and reassuring.

"The doctor said he took the tumor out and you'll probably come home next week."

"Was it malignant?" (The physician should have already told him this.)

"Yes, he said it was malignant, but he wants to start chemotherapy on Monday and you'll only have to come in overnight until he sees how each treatment goes."

Honesty coupled with reassurance is far better for all concerned than the elaborate play-acting in some hospital rooms when patient and visitor pretend the other does not know and each tries to conceal the truth from the other.

In general, the patient ought to know. At least, he should know as much as he wants to know, as much as he can absorb at that time.

Often the diagnosis will have a greater impact upon the family than upon the patient. He heard what the doctor said, but right now is more concerned with the discomfort from surgery, and with being weak and dizzy and confined to the hospital when he would much rather be at work or at home or out on the golf course.

Those close to the patient can help by giving him information at the rate he can accept, remembering that while he may say, "I want to know everything," there are times when he wishes he knew nothing about his illness at all.

My wife's mother developed a heaviness in her side, which was finally diagnosed as cancer. Should we tell Mom? The family had promised Mom before her surgery that there would be no lies afterward; we would not withhold the truth, no matter how devastating.

Autumn's sister, Lila, is a registered nurse. Autumn and her sisters and their father all went into the hospital room and briefly and simply told Mom what the doctor had found. There were tears, and hugs, and more tears, more difficult because the room was only a semi-private.

The two girls left the room so that Dad and Mom could be as alone as possible for a few moments. The two of them had a good cry and said some special things to each other. During the next eighteen months they shared a deeper relationship than they had known before, even during a good marriage, a relationship based upon trust and truth and love, unhindered by the constant need to cover up and maintain secrecy.

Keep in Touch

One of the most important ways we can help someone cope with illness and approaching death is to keep up our relationship with him. Too often friends stay away because they are unsure of what to say. Sometimes even medical people avoid contact with the terminally ill, leaving the patient to deal not only with a frightening illness but with loneliness too.

"What shall we talk about?" Talk about the normal things: family, work, school, football, friends. Talk about anything.

Just because the patient is sick we shouldn't act as if he had quit living. We sometimes consign the terminally ill to the grave prema-

---

*It takes so little effort to
make such a big difference.
—Carol, student nurse, dying*

---

turely. They are still very much alive, often with a heightened capacity to savor pleasant conversation.

"What if he says something about his illness?" What if he does? Go ahead and talk about it, following the rule mentioned above: *Let the patient lead.*

Marie talked openly about her leukemia, about chemotherapy and her body's erratic response to it, and about approaching death. But she also talked about her family, about the neighborhood, about events in her church.

When the disease has progressed to the point where the patient is bedfast and weak, it is still important to visit. You may not need to stay as long, but the few moments you spend there may be the high point of that day for your friend. Nor is it always necessary to talk.

Picture yourself in a hospital room, alone. You are groggy from the medication, but the pain is still there. It comes and goes, like the nurse who checks in every two hours for BP and temps.

Your doctor was in this morning—or was it yesterday—with a couple of new faces you hadn't seen before. The preacher came, said a few words about God, prayed, and was gone.

Visiting hours last night were a disaster. You didn't know if they knew; they didn't know if you knew, and everybody was afraid to say anything and more afraid to be silent.

If only someone would just sit there and be close. If only someone would understand.

Some hospitals and care centers employ trained personnel to work with terminal patients. J. William Worden describes several areas where such persons can help.

The therapist can help the patient manage difficult feelings he or she may be experiencing, such as fear, anger, and sadness.

The therapist can act as an effective link between the family and the medical staff during those times when communication becomes difficult.

The therapist can assure the patient that he or she will have the presence of an understanding person with him or her until the end.

The therapist can help the patient understand his or her feelings of guilt and unfulfillment and help the patient complete emotionally unfinished business he or she may have.

Then Worden adds, "A sensitive, concerned family member who takes the time to learn how to help his dying loved one can be as helpful as a professional therapist."[2]

What does Worden mean by "unfinished business"? He is talking about things the dying patient wants to say to others, broken relationships he or she wants to mend, forgiveness he or she wants to ask, and spiritual matters he or she wants to complete before death. Sometimes there is literal business: a debt to pay, a sale or a purchase, repairs to be made.

Sometimes the pain of an old quarrel or the anguish of a broken relationship is as difficult to bear as the illness. The knowledge that you are away from God can be as frightening on your deathbed as your illness. We perform a genuine service for our loved one if we can enable him to care for his "unfinished business."

A caring family may be able to open a door for God into the patient's heart, a door that was never opened until now. Helpfulness may be a simple, "Remember, Dad, when you taught me to say,

2. J William Worden, PDA—Personal Death Awareness (Englewood Cliffs, NJ: Prentice-Hall, Inc., 1976), p. 86.

'Now I lay me down to sleep'? I'd like to have a prayer with you now if it's okay." Or it may be making arrangements for the patient's baptism.

Every hospital and nearly every care facility has large therapy tanks and the accompanying lifts and equipment to help the patient into and out of the water. Often a staff member will gladly assist, helping the patient dry himself and dress afterward. Usually all that is necessary is for the patient or the family to speak with the attending physician. If the hospital has a chaplain's office, the people there can be most helpful.

Here also the rule is *let the patient lead.* In speaking of spiritual matters, are you trying to salve your own guilt or sense

---

We want to help the patient achieve the best life possible in the time he has remaining.

---

of responsibility, or to bring solace and peace to the patient? We might accomplish more if we listened more and spoke less, even at the bedside of someone terminally ill.

This same sensitivity to the other's needs carries over into the everyday schedule for the patient.

Suppose your mother becomes seriously ill. Everyone in the family immediately pitches in and helps with the dishes, does the housework, goes after the groceries, and tries to shield her from the inevitable problems that arise in a household. In the short term this can help, but be careful. If you take away too much, you deprive her of meaning. Are you telling her that she has nothing to contribute? No one likes to feel useless.

As far as possible, include the patient in the ordinary routines of the family, perhaps taking over the heavier chores but still permitting her to do the dishes or prune the roses or write the checks.

Suppose the patient is a child, maybe your little brother or sister. The time will come soon enough when he or she will have to be hospitalized. For now, one's own bed and usual place at the table will do as much good as the best medicine.

Try not to shut out the patient even when the conversation turns to a discussion of his treatment and care. A family can show love and concern even then, and not make their loved one feel guilt or shame because he is a burden. Let him see that you love him and are happy in helping him.

Young children are usually more disturbed by the thought of leaving parents and family than about dying itself. A brother or sister can, just by being there, assure the dying child that he or she is not alone and will not be abandoned.

Researchers have found that patients who maintain strong ties with their families, and whose families support and comfort them, will live longer than patients who tend to withdraw into themselves, who sink into depression and give up.

In the words of Dr. Carl Simonton, a Dallas radiation oncologist, "We emphasize the concept that all of us *participate* in our health"[3] (emphasis his).

Medical advances have brought us many benefits, but may also create new problems.

In a case described in the journal, *New Physician,* a team of doctors suggested to the parents of twin sons that one of the babies, severely asphyxiated and brain damaged during the difficult birth, be taken off the respirator which had kept him alive for three days. They reacted with intense anger and hostility. Nine days later the baby died, still attached to the machine.

The same doctor told of a second family who sadly accepted the advice to have their child taken off the respirator. This mother wanted to hold her baby until its heart stopped, and the doctors permitted her to come into the neonatal intensive care unit while they took away the tubes and disconnected the respirator.

"She wrapped the child in a blanket and went to sit quietly in a corner for about three hours," the doctor recalls. The baby died in her arms.[4]

This kind of dilemma is not confined to helpless babies. Helpless adults can be subjected to the same thing. What should be done when every medical test shows no brain activity? Should Uncle John be kept on the respirator? If his heart stops, must the "code blue" team come running?

Deep in the back of Uncle John's mind may be the fear that "I'll be put on that machine and kept alive after I'm dead." Family members—and Uncle John—may want to discuss such "heroic measures" with their doctors.

3. Dr. Carl Simonton, in "The Will to Live: Dr. Carl Simonton's Controversial Approach to Cancer Treatment," *D Magazine,* April 1983, p. 120.

4. Marilyn Dunlap, "Today's Dilemma: Live or Let Die?", *Toronto Star,* Monday, March 26, 1983, p. B 1.

Other fears of terminal patients: becoming a burden, losing one's dignity and needing personal care like an infant, pain, loss of appearance, and of course, separation from family, friends, and the only world one has known.

Kathy, on a tour of the Soviet Union, asked her Intourist guide, "Why don't you believe in God?"

"I don't believe in God," the guide answered in perfect but accented English, "because of the way my mother died. She developed cancer, and if there is a God, why did she have to die in the manner she did?"

Gently Kathy responded, "I understand, because my mother had cancer, too. But it was our faith in God that held us together and kept us going all through her sickness. Mother knew she was going to die, and she knew and we knew that after her pain was over, she would be in Heaven with Jesus. You see, Jesus helps us face even something as terrible as that."

Think It Over

1. What specific actions can a family take to assure a dying loved one of their concern and care?

2. What services can a church provide for those within the congregation who suffer from a terminal illness?

3. How can the church help families of the terminally ill?

4. Is your church doing enough now to prepare persons in the congregation for the possibility of life-threatening illness in the family, or in the individual? What ought to be done?

If there is a hell... I'd better know so I can avoid it. It may not be safe to die.
—Maurice Rawlings, M.D.[1]

Does the Future Have a Dark Side?

Not many gas stations are open at three o'clock in the morning, so Barry was glad when he saw the big Shell sign and pulled off the Interstate. Even before he shut off the car, he sensed that something was wrong.

There was nobody around. The station lights were on, the lights were on in the cashier's office, but the place was deserted.

Barry got out of the car and slowly walked toward the cashier's office, glancing around to be sure no one was behind him. Then he saw it, the broken glass and the papers strewn over the floor.

And the blood.

Barry turned and ran to his car and drove until he found a phone and called the police. The police found two bodies, both shot in the face; the night attendant and a friend who had told his parents he was going over to the station to see his buddy.

The killer? Twenty-three, he already had a long record. Twice he had been in trouble over narcotics, the second time coupled with an armed robbery charge. He was back on the streets because his lawyers had worked out a plea-bargain deal in exchange for info on a county-wide drug ring.

1. Maurice Rawlings, M.D., *Before Death Comes* (Nashville, Thomas Nelson Publishers, 1980), p. 119. Used by permission.

On their first date, Jim heard Sherry's scream and saw the lights at the same moment, but it was too late. At ninety miles an hour the drunk slammed into their car.

Beautiful Sherry died instantly. They kept her casket closed during calling hours and the funeral.

Mealtimes are worst for Jim. Paralyzed, he can smell his mother's cooking but would choke if she were to feed him. They keep him alive through a tube into his stomach.

The drunk? Unhurt, he ran from the scene. When an officer said, "Do you know you killed a girl back there?" he shrugged and responded, "So?"

It may be a question in the minds of some whether there is any punishment of sin, either in this world or in the world to come.
        —*J.W. McGarvey, preaching in Lexington, Kentucky, June 11, 1893*[2]

What about the twenty-eight-year-old neighbor who, instead of taking little Christa to school that day, drove her to a lonely road, dragged her into the woods, raped her, strangled her to death, and left her body to rot?

Or the guy who locks the door to his room and gets out the girlie mags and crawls over the pages with his eyes? Or the student who cheats through school? Or the person with the raunchy mouth? Or the porno crowd?

What about yourself? Maybe you've never robbed or shot someone, but what about those things you've done that you'd hate to have anyone find out? What about the things you've done wrong?

Does God Ignore Sin?

How has God set up His world? What happens to those who do wrong?

Because they sinned, Adam and Eve had to leave the garden (Genesis 3:22-24). Murderous Cain refused to accept his guilt over killing Abel, then tried to avoid the consequences, telling God, "My punishment is more than I can bear" (Genesis 4:13). But he did not escape it.

---

2. J.W. McGarvey, *Sermons* (Cincinnati, Standard Publishing Company, 1894), p. 17.

The flood swept away an evil civilization (Genesis 6:7); wicked Sodom and Gomorrah perished in catastrophe (Genesis 18:20, 21; 19:24-29); Moses' wrath barred him from the promised land (Numbers 20:3-13; Deuteronomy 3:23-27; 34:1-6).

God does not ignore sin. Knowing what would happen to unbelieving Jerusalem brought Jesus to tears (Luke 19:41-44). Paul's analysis of sin's results remains accurate today:

> They exchanged the truth of God for a lie, and worshiped and served created things rather than the Creator—who is forever praised. Amen.
> Because of this, God gave them over to shameful lusts. Even their women exchanged natural relations for unnatural ones. In the same way the men also abandoned natural relations with women and were inflamed with lust for one another. Men committed indecent acts with other men, and received in themselves the due penalty for their perversion.
> —Romans 1:25-28

God punishes sin. In this life, God punishes sin. Not even nations are exempt. Witness the ruin of Hitler's Third Reich.

Individuals also come to ruin, swiftly or slowly. It is not merely that a criminal is jailed or a wild driver is maimed or a glutton gets the gout. Many sins are not so obvious, and punishment comes in subtle ways.

Sin is deadly. Pick up a salacious novel and read the "juicy" parts. You've programmed vivid video into your mind, which turns God's holy merging of male and female into something cheap and trashy, often with a twist of cruelty or violence. And how these images last!

Learn to swear, and overnight you'll find that your new habit is nearly impossible to break.

Punishment for sin? It's everywhere, isn't it? In loss of self-respect. In guilt. In the slow erosion of character. Our health, even our mental state, is affected by sin.

Sin is cancer of the soul. No wonder we lack the spiritual power to live our best. No wonder we constantly have to pick ourselves up and start again. And it's not always from falling. Too often we jump.

Still we are disturbed because punishment seems unequal. Some people suffer acutely for small sins, while conscienceless sinners seem to prosper. Perhaps they suffer in ways we do not know. But is earthly punishment all there is?

Is There Any Punishment After This Life Is Over?

Jesus selected twelve men to be His apostles. He knew they faced danger. He knew the road would not be easy. As He gave them their instructions, He also knew they would be afraid, so He included this warning:

> Do not be afraid of those who kill the body but cannot kill the soul. Rather, be afraid of the one who can destroy both soul and body in hell.
>
> —Matthew 10:28

On the south side of Jerusalem lay the city dump where people burned their trash. It had not always been that. King Ahaz worshiped idols and set up images in that area, which then was called the Valley of Ben Hinnom. He even sacrificed some of his own children there (2 Chronicles 28:3). Manasseh, another king, did the same (2 Chronicles 33:1-9).

The word *hell* used here is a translation of the Greek *Geenna* or *Gehenna*. This seems to be a Hebrew word carried over into Greek. Thayer tells us the name is derived from a word meaning lamentation, and the place is so called from the cries of little children who were sacrificed and thrown into the fiery arms of Moloch, an idol in the form of a bull.[3]

King Josiah was determined to banish idol worship of all kinds. He desecrated the Valley of Ben Hinnom so it would not be used for worship (2 Kings 23:10). Probably that was when the place became the city dump. Not only trash, but dead animals and the bodies of criminals were thrown there to be burned or devoured by dogs.

This must have been the worst place in the vicinity of Jerusalem, and Jesus used its name for the eternal fate of the wicked. If He were talking to us today, maybe He would use the word *Incinerator.*

Have you ever burned papers or garbage in an incinerator? We used to have one that burned so hot the metal chimney glowed red and the fire made a whooshing sound. Standing several feet away you could feel the heat.

It is as if Jesus were saying, "If you'd be afraid of being thrown into an incinerator, be more afraid of what will happen if you turn away from God."

---

3. Thayer's *Greek-English Lexicon of the New Testament.*

If There Is Punishment After Death,
When Does It Begin?

As much at home in the next world as in this, Jesus gives us a preview of the world to come.

> There was a rich man who was dressed in purple and fine linen and lived in luxury every day. At his gate was laid a beggar named Lazarus, covered with sores and longing to eat what fell from the rich man's table. Even the dogs came and licked his sores.
>
> The time came when the beggar died and the angels carried him to Abraham's side. The rich man also died and was buried. In hell, where he was in torment, he looked up and saw Abraham far away, with Lazarus by his side. So he called to him, "Father Abraham, have pity on me and send Lazarus to dip the tip of his finger in water and cool my tongue, because I am in agony in this fire."
>
> —Luke 16:19-24

Concerned with getting the best in this world, the rich man never thought of the next. What happened when he died? He went immediately to an awful place, "in torment" so terrible that he begged for even a drop of water.

The man knew where he was, recognized Lazarus, could see and talk and feel; but there was none of the soft indulgence he had known before. "I am in agony in this fire," he said (Luke 16:24).

The worst part of all was knowing that he didn't have to be there! Had he listened to the Scripture, he would never have gone to that tormenting place. (See verse 29.) But now it was too late. There was no going back.

Incidentally, the word *hell* in verse 23 is a different word from the one used in Matthew 10:28. There the word is *gehenna;* here it is *hades,* which literally means *not to be seen.*

We say *the hereafter;* they said *the unseen,* where people—not their bodies but their spirits—went after they died.

The rich man found that in Hades he was separated—forever separated—from anything good or anyone good. Nor could Abraham help him. Lazarus couldn't help either. The rich man couldn't help himself. His situation was hopeless.

There would never be any relief. Never.

Not ever.

If Punishment Begins After People Die,
What About the Judgment?

It is almost amazing to find out how much Jesus says about what happens to those who disobey God.

> Woe to you, Korazin! Woe to you, Bethsaida! ... It will be more bearable for Tyre and Sidon on the day of judgment than for you. And you, Capernaum ... it will be more bearable for Sodom on the day of judgment than for you.
> —Matthew 11:21-24

> I tell you that men will have to give account on the day of judgment for every careless word they have spoken.
> —Matthew 12:36

> The men of Nineveh will stand up at the judgment with this generation and condemn it; for they repented at the preaching of Jonah, and now one greater than Jonah is here. The Queen of the South will rise at the judgment with this generation and condemn it; for she came from the ends of the earth to listen to Solomon's wisdom, and now one greater than Solomon is here.
> —Matthew 12:41, 42

The Day of Judgment, then, will be a day when "this generation" and "the Queen of the South" and "the men of Nineveh" and those who have spoken "every careless word" and the people of Tyre and Sidon and Sodom and Korazin and Capernaum and Bethsaida will all be there! And every person will give an account of what he has done. For some it will be "more bearable." Less so for others.

---

*I regret my sins. What I regret most is
that I do not regret them more.*

Paul describes it this way:

> For we must all appear before the judgment seat of Christ, that each one may receive what is due him for the things done while in the body, whether good or bad.
> —2 Corinthians 5:10

119

Are you ready to receive what is due you for the things you are doing while in the body? Kind of stops you in your tracks, doesn't it?

Let's go on. Jesus knew how it would sound when He talked about the judgment, but He kept talking about it because He wanted people to be ready:

> Do not be amazed at this, for a time is coming when all who are in their graves will hear his voice [the voice of the Son of God] and come out—those who have done good will rise to live, and those who have done evil will rise to be condemned.
> —John 5:28, 29

Less than a week before His death Jesus was still teaching about the time when "all the nations will be gathered before him, and he will separate the people one from another as a shepherd separates the sheep from the goats" (Matthew 25:32).

So it's coming. Someday in the future—perhaps tomorrow, perhaps years from now, perhaps when we have to be brought back from the dead to be present—someday you and I and everyone else will stand before God. Probably the clearest description of what it will be like is found in the Book of Revelation.

> Then I saw a great white throne and him who was seated on it. Earth and sky fled from his presence, and there was no place for them. And I saw the dead, great and small, standing before the throne, and books were opened. Another book was opened, which is the book of life. The dead were judged according to what they had done as recorded in the books. The sea gave up the dead that were in it, and death and Hades gave up the dead that were in them, and each person was judged according to what he had done. Then death and Hades were thrown into the lake of fire. The lake of fire is the second death. If anyone's name was not found written in the book of life, he was thrown into the lake of fire.
> —Revelation 20:11-15

Does Punishment End With Judgment?

From that grim picture the scene changes to one of the loveliest word pictures in all language. Instead of a "lake of fire," we see "a new heaven and a new earth." Dread of judgment is gone. There is no dread of anything.

Now the dwelling of God is with men, and he will live with them. They will be his people, and God himself will be with them and be their God. He will wipe every tear from their eyes.　　　　　　　　　　　　—Revelation 21:3, 4

But not everyone is there.

The cowardly, the unbelieving, the vile, the murderers, the sexually immoral, those who practice magic arts, the idolaters and all liars—their place will be in the fiery lake of burning sulphur. This is the second death.

　　　　　　　　　　　　　　　　　—Revelation 21:8

For how long?

For as long as Heaven is.

For as long as God rewards those who are His own. Look again at the words of Jesus: "Then they will go away to eternal punishment, but the righteous to eternal life" (Matthew 25:46).

How long will the righteous enjoy the reward of their service? "Eternal!" How long will the wicked be punished? The word is the same: "Eternal!"

In *The First Circle,* Solzhenitsyn tells about Innokenty Volodin, a State Counselor in the USSR's Ministry of Foreign Affairs. Suddenly arrested, Volodin is torn away from his home, his wife, his career; stripped of his post, his medals, and his uniform.

Thrown into the Lubyanka, Volodin, sleepless and exhausted, is fingerprinted and registered as a prisoner. He shudders as he sees the paper they lay in front of him. Above the fingerprints is written, "Volodin, Innokenty Artemyevich, 1919, Leningrad." Over that, in thick, bold type, are the words, "KEEP FOREVER."

Isn't this the way it will be in hell: KEEP FOREVER? Imagine what it will be like: KEEP FOREVER.

Does God Have to Punish?

Go back to those horrible examples—every one true—we looked at earlier. That young man who drove to the North Canton Shell and killed two people, then took broken glass and nearly cut one boy's head off—he would not have been free had not the judge turned him loose. Unpunished, he was able to murder, and did.

The drunk who smashed poor Sherry to death and ruined Jim's life had been in court *repeatedly* for drunk driving. Where were the lawyers who got him off? Maybe they ought to stand at Jim's bedside and help his mother feed and bathe and care for him.

Ask Jim's mother if she thinks drunken drivers should be punished. This is not a matter of revenge; it is a matter of safety for those who use cars and highways properly.

Do you think the man who raped and killed the little girl ought to go free?

God *has* to punish. What if He permitted evil to go right along with good forever?

It is for this very reason that hell exists: to take everything that is bad away, and keep it forever away from the good.

Sadly Terry remembers her grandfather:

> He had no time for God or Christ. He never went to church. He had been sick, so he knew he was dying. He kept screaming, "My bed is on fire. Help, there is a fire in my bed. I can't stand it. Get me out of here. There is fire in my bed and I am burning." And then he died.

Is that how you want to die?

Neither do I. If we go to hell, of all the terrible things about that awful place, the worst will be knowing we didn't have to go there.

Jesus said, "I hold the keys of death and Hades" (Revelation 1:18).

Have you accepted Him?

For Further Research

Our English word *hell* is used to translate four different words in the Bible. *Gehenna* and *Hades* have been mentioned in this chapter. *Sheol* is often used in the Old Testament.

Sometimes translated "the grave," *Sheol* is the name the Hebrews gave to the place the dead people are. The New Testament word *Hades* is similar. *Sheol* in Psalm 16:10 is *Hades* when the verse is quoted in Acts 2:27.

Tartarus is a name used in Greek mythology, but in the Bible it is the name of a real place. While *Hades* is a general term for the abode of the dead, *Tartarus* means specifically the place of the wicked spirits. In the Bible it is seen only in 2 Peter 2:4.

You may want to look at ways the words are used:

Sheol: 2 Samuel 22:6; Job 11:8; Psalm 18:5; Proverbs 7:27; Isaiah 5:14; and others.

Hades: Matthew 11:23; 16:18; Revelation 6:8; and others.

Gehenna: Matthew 5:22, 29; 23:15, 33; Mark 9:43-48; James 3:6; and others.

Think It Over

1. Check into your local newspaper and see if there is a story about someone who is trying to avoid being punished, or who in some way has avoided punishment. Ask a friend what he or she thinks about the story.

2. After reading Revelation 21:8, how might you answer a person who tells you, "I really don't think it matters much whether you believe in God or not"?

3. Can you write your own definition of hell?

If you read history, you will find that the Christians who did the most for the present world were just those who thought most of the next.

—C.S. Lewis

Four Views on What's Coming

Pick up a newspaper and it doesn't take long to discover how interested people are in the future. Whether it is some political pundit prognosticating, or a market analyst talking bulls and bears, or an astrologist mouthing elaborate nonsense, it gets read.

A considerable portion of the public seems willing to give almost anything to know what's going to happen tomorrow, and smooth operators can make a comfortable living offering predictions of one kind or another.

The Bible, too, offers predictions, but of a quite different sort from those we see in the paper or hear over nighttime radio. Let's examine four views, by four separate individuals, given at different times and under different circumstances, and see what they said about the future.

We'll hear first from Jesus.

The Future: I'm Going Away, But I'll Come Back for You
John 14:1-6

Has any Scripture, with the possible exception of the Twenty-third Psalm, been read at so many funerals as these words of Jesus: "Do not let your hearts be troubled. Trust in God; trust also in me"? (John 14:1).

Not too long ago I was summoned to a home by the tragic death of a sixteen-year-old boy on a motorcycle. My heart went out to those parents, numb with shock and grief, the father pacing the floor in silence, the mother sitting on the couch looking through one of those oversized Bibles sold door to door.

"Tell me," she sobbed, "that my boy is with Jesus. Show me in this Bible where it says he is with Jesus."

She had heard that message before and she wanted to hear it again. Here in John 14 is one place where she could find it.

The Speaker. Our speaker is Jesus Christ, the Son of God. You and I cannot see over the next hill; He can see eternity. Regarding tomorrow, we guess and hope; Jesus *knows.*

We lean closer to hear the last words of someone who is dying, not wanting to miss even one. This is Jesus' last talk with His disciples before His death. He knows that by this time tomorrow He will be dead and buried. Every word is important.

The Audience. Jesus is speaking to eleven of the twelve men He selected to be His apostles. Judas has left on his treacherous errand (John 13:30). Jesus sees the uncertainty and tension on every face. These men know Jesus' enemies are plotting against Him. Jesus wants to assure them that all is not lost. What will happen tomorrow, when they see Him scourged and crucified? How will they ever stand that?

There is only one way. Jesus points them to what will come afterward, to His ultimate victory and theirs. He tells them of a world without death or suffering or pain or terror.

The Time. This is the night before Jesus' betrayal, trial, crucifixion, and death.

The Message. Jesus speaks of going and coming back. "My Father's house," with its "many rooms," is different from the world in which they are eating and talking.

Jesus speaks of "a place." He is not trying to picture some vague spiritual limbo. He is going to a place and will come back for the disciples and take them to that place.

The place involves preparation. This will be no quick and easy task. Preparing the way and preparing the place involve Jesus personally. Count the number of times Jesus uses "me" or "I" or "my" in these verses.

Wherever the place is, Jesus is crucial in getting there. He tells Thomas and the others, "No one comes to the Father except through me" (John 14:6).

All this is so that they "may be where I am." Jesus wanted them to be with Him and Him to be with them. Wherever that place is and whatever else it is, it means being with Jesus.

Jesus promises a place where His disciples will be with Him forever, in His Father's house. He wants them to know so that they will not be afraid.

The Future: All Christians, Living and Dead, Will Be With Jesus Forever
1 Thessalonians 4:13-18

The Speaker. The speaker here is the apostle Paul, a persecutor who became a preacher. Paul came to Thessalonica on his second missionary journey, after God called him to "come over to Macedonia" (Acts 16:9). Paul's policy was to go to chief cities first, since both need and opportunity were greatest there.

The Audience. Paul writes to the church in Thessalonica, a port city on the Aegean, ideally situated on a protected arm of the sea and a main east-west highway. Thessalonica was an important city. A European city, too. From here, the church could reach the Mediterranean world and beyond.

Paul was not given much time in Thessalonica. He had been there only three weeks when some unbelieving Jews incited a mob against him, and he and Silas were forced to flee (Acts 17:1-10).

Nonetheless, a church was formed, and this little group "became a model to all the believers in Macedonia and Achaia" (1 Thessalonians 1:7). Their influence was considerable. Paul said that from them the message of the Lord rang out not only in Macedonia and Achaia, that is, the peninsula now known as Greece, but "your faith in God has become known everywhere" (1 Thessalonians 1:8).

They had turned from idols to serve the living God. They were waiting for Jesus to come from Heaven. And it was this waiting for Christ's return that had caused some problems.

Some of their group had died. What had happened to them? Did they, because they were dead, lose their hope of seeing Jesus come back? Had they, by dying too soon, lost their reward as Christians?

Paul wrote to explain what was going to happen.

The Time. First Thessalonians is Paul's earliest letter, and perhaps the first book of the New Testament ever written. Wanting to know how things were in Thessalonica, Paul sent Timothy to see, and to encourage the Christians there (1 Thessalonians 3:2-6). Timothy returned with good news about the faith and love of the Thessalonian Christians, and Paul then wrote his first letter to them.

This letter is especially interesting because it opens a window into the beliefs of the church at an early time, possibly even before any of the New Testament had been written.

You ask, "Why doesn't God do something about death?" He has.

The Message. Paul doesn't hesitate. He wants them to know. Just as Jesus rose from the dead, those who died in Him will rise. When Jesus comes back, they will come back with Him. Death has not robbed them of their reward, nor will we who are still living when Jesus returns have any advantage over those who died in Him.

Our Lord will come as He promised and call the dead to life (John 5:25-29). Then all of us who belong to Him will be caught up to meet Him. Nothing will ever be able to separate us from Him.

Paul's key thought is "in Christ." If we are "in Christ" here, we will be "in Christ" hereafter. Living or dead, we are in Him.

Paul is saying, "When you carry your dead to the graveyard, when you feel your own strength ebbing and know death is near, do not grieve as those who have no hope. Take heart!

"We will be with the Lord forever," he writes. "Therefore encourage each other with these words" (1 Thessalonians 4:17, 18).

The Future: the World as We Know It Will Pass Away
2 Peter 3:3-14

The Speaker. Simon Peter was one of the very first to follow Jesus (John 1:40-42). Jesus spent time in his house (Mark 1:29-34), let him see and hear more than some others (Mark 5:37-42; Matthew 14:28-33; 17:1-8). Peter knew who Jesus was (Matthew 16:16; John 6:66-69). As a leader in the early church, he endured intense persecution and courageously witnessed to Jesus' resurrection (Acts 4:3-20; 5:27-42).

The Audience. Peter's first letter was to Christians facing persecution. His second seems more general, directed "to those who through the righteousness of our God and Savior Jesus Christ have received a faith as precious as ours" (2 Peter 1:1). This letter might be directed to us.

127

The Time. This letter is much later than 1 Thessalonians. Peter knows that he will die soon (2 Peter 1:13, 14). His writing lets us see what the church believed and taught after considerable time had passed, after the gospel had spread across the Mediterranean world, after persecution and death had taken many Christians.

The Message. The time will come, Peter tells us, when people will scoff at the idea of Jesus' second coming. Having closed their minds to the facts concerning the flood (Genesis 6—8), these unbelievers will not accept the idea that someday the world will end. They say, "Everything goes on as it has since the beginning of creation." Therefore they suppose everything will always go on in the same way and not be interrupted by Jesus' return.

Dr. John Wesley White, a Canadian evangelist, told an audience in Toronto of an experience he had with a teacher in high school.

> It was my first serious attempt to witness. Before I could hardly get started, the teacher took my Bible and turned to 2 Peter 3:12 and read where the elements would be destroyed. "Don't you know," the teacher taunted me, "that matter can neither be created nor destroyed? When you find a way to either create matter or to destroy it, then you can come back and talk to me."
>
> Well, that was before the atomic bomb. We saw over Hiroshima and Nagasaki what happens when its energy is released and matter is destroyed.

Peter's description reads as if he were an eyewitness. Does this mean the end will come in an atomic war? Not necessarily.

Remember the Periodic Table of the Elements? In creation, God simply arranged energy. An atom is a carefully balanced unit of energy. Scientists have found a way to unbalance certain atoms and release some of their energy. But it was God who organized energy in creation; and if He so chooses, He will be the one to release it in the destruction of the world. Peter's description is so accurate as to be horrifying (2 Peter 3:10).

But the Christian will be spared, saved, in keeping with God's promise. "We are looking forward to a new heaven and a new earth, the home of righteousness" (2 Peter 3:13). What a tremendous motivation to do our best! What a challenge! What hope! "Since you are looking forward to this, make every effort to be found spotless, blameless and at peace with him" (2 Peter 3:14).

The Future: Joy and Peace
in the Presence of Our God
Revelation 7:9-17

The Speaker. Our fourth speaker is the apostle John, probably one of the first-day followers of Jesus (John 1:35-40). For a lifetime John followed the Master, close to Him in life (John 13:23), in His death (John 19:26), and after the resurrection (John 20:1-9; 21:1-7, 20).

Because of his prominence as a Christian leader, the authorities exiled John to Patmos, an island off the coast of Asia Minor. While John was on Patmos, God permitted him to see the future.

The Audience. The imperial persecutions had begun. Under Nero, Christians were "nailed on crosses; others sewn up in the skins of wild beasts, and exposed to the fury of dogs; others again, smeared with combustible materials, were used as torches to illuminate the darkness of the night."[1]

Later emperors continued to devastate the church. Some of those to whom John wrote could name people who had gone to their deaths for Christ. All of them faced that threat.

The Time. How did Jesus see the future? We looked at John 14. In the early days, how did the church see it? First Thessalonians 4 gives us our answer. Years later, after the new faith had spread, when the possibility of persecution was hanging over the church, what did they

For Further Research

The word *tribulation* in Revelation 7:14 has the root idea of *a pressing* or *pressing together* or *pressure.*[2]

You'll be interested in other ways the Greek word is used and translated. In these quotations the words in italics are all translations of the same Greek word.

"In this world you will have *trouble,*" said Jesus (John 16:33). Paul speaks of Christ's comfort in "all our *troubles*" (2 Corinthians 1:4).

Stephen referred to the famine in Canaan and the *"great suffering"* it brought (Acts 7:11). Paul explained to the Corinthians that he did not want them to give and be *"hard pressed,* but that there might be equality" (2 Corinthians 8:13).

James indicated that genuine religion is "to look after orphans and widows in their *distress*" (James 1:27).

---

1. Edward Gibbon, *The Decline and Fall of the Roman Empire* (New York, The Modern Library, no date given,) volume I, p. 457.

2. Thayer's Lexicon.

still believe about the future? Second Peter gives us that word.

In each case we saw that Jesus and His people looked to the future with confidence and hope, even though they expected to face persecution and they knew the earth itself would be destroyed.

Now, later still, with thousands tortured and killed, with many more imprisoned and persecuted, did the church have any faith left in the future?

These four representative passages give us a panoramic view of the continuing and unfading confidence Jesus and His followers had concerning coming events. This passage, Revelation 7, was written toward the close of John's life, possibly in the last year of the reign of Emperor Domitian, A.D. 96.

It wasn't ethics or moralizing that swept across the ancient world; it was the news that Jesus had come out of His grave alive again and that, through Him, anyone who wanted to could do the same.

The Message. At the point of our need, God always supplies. When Israel could stand it no longer, Moses was sent. During "the dark ages" in Israel, it was Elijah. Jesus came "when the time had fully come" (Galatians 4:4).

Before A.D. 96, the church has weathered storms of persecution. Now with more dark clouds on the horizon, God sends His message of promise and hope. John takes us into God's very presence, shows us God's throne, lets us hear the celestial choir and meet the angels.

One of the elders asks John to identify the great crowd gathered from every tribe and nation and people and language, but John cannot.

"Sir," he answers, "you know." In other words, you tell me.

The elder explains that these are those whom God has delivered out of great suffering, and that they stand here cleansed by the blood of Christ. Years before, on the banks of the Jordan, John heard Jesus introduced as "the Lamb of God, who takes away the sin of the world" (John 1:29, 36).

What is it like to serve God in Heaven? Sometimes we're embarrassed here by our pitiful attempts for God, but not in Heaven. There they know the solid satisfaction of excellence; there is nothing second-rate. God's grace makes up all our deficiencies. If we have failed on earth we shall succeed in Heaven; but if we have been proud of our small successes here we shall be humble in greater achievements there. We shall know that all things are of God, and to Him we shall give the glory.

Jesus' life, that holy life given on the cross and brought back from the grave, flows through their lives now. Lifted above hunger and thirst and fatigue and hesitation, they can offer God service worthy of Him.

Their robes are pure, their hearts are pure, their service is pure. There is none of the jealousy and pride and false motives that sometimes mar our service here.

They will be close to God, and God will be close to them. In that Eastern setting John expressed that closeness in terms they would understand:

> He who sits on the throne will
>   spread his tent over them.
> Never again will they hunger;
>   never again will they thirst.
> The sun will not beat upon them,
>   nor any scorching heat.
> —Revelation 7:15, 16

In our culture we might say, "God will put His arms around us and see that nothing happens to hurt us."

Tears? No tears there. The Lord, the Lamb who has become the Shepherd, will be their Friend, and they will be His forever. What does it matter if we do not understand all the eloquent language of Revelation? We understand that we will be with the Jesus and He will take care of us. It is enough.

We look at some who saw Jesus on earth and wonder how they could not accept Him, especially the Jews who had the Old Testament predictions of what His coming would be like. When we get to Heaven we will look back and see the Scriptures and wonder why we did not understand them better and know more completely the joy of being with God. It is as Isaiah wrote and Paul quoted,

> No eye has seen,
>   no ear has heard,
> no mind has conceived
>   what God has prepared for those who love him.
> —Isaiah 64:4; 1 Corinthians 2:9

131

The Future: What Will It Be
for Us?

The Speaker. In our high-decibel world someone is constantly shouting at us. It's a wonder we can hear ourselves think. Back of this high-tech din the voice of God speaks. It speaks through God's Son and through His chosen spokesmen who are inspired by the Holy Spirit, and we read its message in the Scriptures.

With one voice Peter and Paul and John and our Lord Jesus himself unite to say that a there is another world after this. "Don't give up," they tell us, "because what God has prepared for His people is better than anything here."

The Audience. We are God's audience, we who live under the dubious protection of a "balance of terror," in a world where biological and chemical weapons are stacked alongside nuclear ones, we who are blackmailed by terrorists, and nearly suffocated by hedonism and pornography.

God is speaking to you. God is speaking to me.

God is also speaking to the world in general. To those who think that success is new cars and designer jeans. To those putting their faith in genetic engineering. To those giving up and hiding behind a narcotic screen.

The Time. The time is now. God is speaking to us now. We live in the last days of the 1980s, perhaps in the last days of Planet Earth. For the first time in history, scientists and anthropologists and historians and political figures and biologists are seriously discussing the end of life as we know it.

The Message. Does God have anything to say to a world facing economic disruption and shifting cultural patterns and depletion of natural resources and increasing deprivation?

Does God have a word for a civilization that may finally realize that man does not have the answer, and that the answer must come from a higher source? Does God have anything to say to this kind of world?

From Jesus we learn that the future holds a place, carefully prepared, for His people, and that He wants to take us there. What is that place like? Like home. Like being at home with God. In the Father's house. Better than the very best home we could have here.

"With the Lord forever," Paul tells us. Those who have gone on and we who are still living when He comes will rise to meet Jesus, and we will be with Him forever. Paul tells us to comfort and encourage each other with this promise.

132

We Christians can't possibly be pessimistic when we remember what God has in store for us. Even if everyone else gives up, we'll still be able to go on, because we know what's ahead.

In awful terms Peter describes the end of the world, when God will "let go" the energy He has held together since creation.

"The heavens will disappear with a roar," he warns. Next to that, an H-bomb would sound like a firecracker. Next to that, Hiroshima would look good.

When is it going to happen? "The Lord is not slow in keeping his promise," Peter emphasizes, ". . . not wanting anyone to perish, but everyone to come to repentance" (2 Peter 3:9).

God is waiting, keeping the door open, hoping for people to come to Jesus and be saved before it is too late. Is He waiting for you?

From Revelation John gives us a glimpse of Heaven, where people from all nations, all times, all languages, will be assembled before God's throne to praise Him forever. I want to be there. How about you?

Jesus is the way, as He said: "I am the way and the truth and the life" (John 14:6). He will show us. He will take us. He will protect us. We shall be safe with Him.

Think It Over

1. Many people see a connection between the cleansing referred to in Revelation 7:14 and baptism. Check into these Scriptures and see what you think: John 3:3-5; Acts 2:38; Romans 6:1-4; Galatians 3:26, 27; Ephesians 5:26; Titus 3:5-7; and 1 Peter 3:21.

2. Take a sheet of paper and put together a composite description of the future, using John 14:1-6, 1 Thessalonians 4:13-18, 2 Peter 3:3-14, and Revelation 7:9-17.

You are not going to an unknown country,
for Christ is there.

—Charles Kingsley[1]

Welcome to the City of Life

There's something fascinating about the city. Stroll down Karntner Strasse in Vienna on a summer evening. Windowshop until you're pleasantly tired of needlepoint and crystal and ceramics and furs. Find a table in one of the sidewalk cafes down Graben and watch the crowds go by.

Drive along the Thames and look across at Parliament House and Big Ben. Think of wave after wave of Luftwaffe bombers trying to destroy all that is here. Ready your camera for Buckingham Palace and the changing of the guard. London! This is London and you don't want to miss anything!

Fly into Washington National. To your left, the Capitol, the Mall, Washington's Monument and Lincoln Memorial. Swallow hard as your mind keeps repeating, "Liberty," and "Freedom," and "Justice for all."

Maybe you prefer Frisco and the cable cars or St. Louis and Gateway Arch or Columbus or Dallas or Portland.

There's something about the city! Music and art and entertainment—you'll find them in the city! Maybe you like Phoenix or Santa Fe or Honolulu. Or maybe you are sure your own home town is the loveliest city of all.

---

1. See *Leaves of Gold* (Williamsport, Pennsylvania, The Coslett Publishing Co., 1962), p. 94.

Exiled on lonely Patmos, John can remember cities where he has been: Capernaum, Ephesus, Jerusalem. Especially Jerusalem! His heart yearns for the Jerusalem he knew when he and Jesus and the others walked the temple courts and climbed the Mount of Olives and crossed the Kidron and prayed in Gethsemane.

Now those days are gone.

John will never walk those streets again, never hear those sounds again, never see those sights again.

God gives John a preview of another Jerusalem, in a new heaven and a new earth. God permits John to see the bride of Christ, new Jerusalem, redeemed and ready for the bridegroom.

Jerusalem, city of the future.

A great city.

The greatest city ever.

What Will Heaven Be Like?

John almost empties the dictionary trying to describe what he saw. What will Heaven be like? It won't be like this world. Heaven will be different. Better. Heaven will be new; nothing second-hand. Nothing worn or wearing out. There will be no rust, no decay. No blight or anything.

How quickly things here lose their newness! You buy a new car and hope it will last until it's paid for. This year's clothes will be out of style next.

That crumbling two-story, infested with roaches and rats, was not always like that. It used to smell of new wood and fresh paint instead of sweat and sour cabbage. Tenants used to be proud of such a good address. But that was years ago.

We too become old and stale. We think, "When I get to college, things will be different." Or, "When I find a job and get out on my own," or "If I had more money."

Sometimes we get bored. Weary. We run out to the mall and find something we want and take it home and think we'll be happy, and how long does it last? An evening? A week? Two weeks?

Sure, we're happy for a while. Until we see something else we want or think we need. Usually something newer.

In Heaven—think of it—our inheritance "can never perish, spoil or fade" (1 Peter 1:4).

Tired of living? Not in Heaven. Heaven will be perennially new, with no garbage dumps, no scrap yards, no pollution control boards.

Heaven will be a planned city, and beautiful. How seldom are our cities *designed*. Usually they just happen, and the results are apparent: urban blight, uncontrolled development, suburban sprawl. We thought "slash and burn" went out with our forebears! What the early settlers did to the piedmont we're doing everywhere.

Look at the size of John's city. Fifteen hundred miles wide and high and long. Compute the volume in that cube!

No crowded tenements in Heaven. No look-alike tract houses. No mass-produced condos with their pressboard cabinets and two-by-four closets.

Heaven will have room for all; space to live and love and serve. Room to *be!* No jostling subway crowds. No traffic jams. No waiting in line.

Heaven's design pictures perfection. In Solomon's temple, the Most Holy Place, symbolic of God's presence, was exactly as high as it was long and as it was wide (1 Kings 6:20). Heaven will be God's perfect dwelling place.

What a city!

Sightseeing in downtown Toronto you wonder if all Canada is as rich. From the CN Tower, over eighteen hundred feet high, to the gilded Royal Bank or elegant Commerce Court or somber Dominion Centre, you keep thinking, "Look at all the money here."

Yet Heaven is richer. Richer than Yonge or Bay Street, richer than Eaton Centre, Imperial Bank, Casa Loma, and Harbourfront put together! All that wealth, plus Wall Street, plus all the Swiss banks, plus OPEC—all of it would not buy one pebble from Main Street, Heaven.

The City of Life

As the shadows lengthen, our cities change. Darkness drives out the daytime crowds, suffocates the city's life and spirit. In our cities night brings emptiness and fear.

No threatening figure lurks in Heaven's shadows, for there is neither threat nor shadow. You won't have to keep glancing over your shoulder in Heaven. You can walk anywhere unafraid, and in all this city of gold and jewels, there is not a "No Trespassing" sign anywhere.

No porno shops in Heaven. No forensic labs. No morgues. No like-new TV's for sale cheap. No whispered offer from someone who won't quite look you in the eye.

No blood banks. No ER's. No wailing sirens. No heart monitors. No cemeteries.

Instead of these trappings of death, there is the water of life. And there is the tree of life, with its healing harvest to soothe and to bless. How we need this healing for life's cuts and bruises!

Some time ago I met a couple from the church at the grocery store and proceeded to tell them about the excitement the night before when a drunken kid ran into two parked cars across the street and woke up the neighborhood.

I threw on clothes over my pajamas and went out to find the boy unhurt and leaning against his car. "Where's my car?" he kept saying, so drunk he couldn't even see it! I laughed as I told the story.

How was I to know that last night their son also had wrecked a car, also drunk, and that they also had been up all night at the hospital and at the jail where the police took their son?

No hurts like theirs in Heaven. No failure to understand like mine in Heaven. No emergency phone calls and no sleepless nights and no heart-stopping crashes in the darkness, for "the old order of things has passed away" (Revelation 21:4).

There is darkness without, and when I die there will be darkness within. There is no splendor, no vastness anywhere; only trivality for a moment, and then nothing.
—Bertrand Russell, unbeliever[2]

What makes your life on earth less than perfect? Whatever it is, there will be none of it in Heaven.

For centuries, man has labored under the shadow of death, seeing friend and family to the grave, feeling death's cold breath chilling him, reminding him of his own mortality. But not in Heaven. Water of life. Tree of life. Book of life. The message is clear: death is gone; life has come. Death is gone. Life has come.

John paints in bold strokes, deliberately selecting from the best of earth and telling us that Heaven will be like that and more: gold and jewels, precious stones and pearls, pure water, abundant light, open gates, joyous freedom.

Heaven will exceed our very best dreams.

---

2. Quoted in David Winter, *Hereafter: What happens after Death* (Wheaton, Harold Shaw Publishers, 1972, 73), p. 5.

For Further Research

It's interesting to see the history of worship and how it is perfected in Heaven.

God met man face to face before sin entered; but after that, worship involved an altar and sacrifice:

Abel (Genesis 4:3, 4)
Noah (Genesis 8:20, 21)
Joshua (Joshua 8:30, 31)

Even in the case of Abraham and Isaac, customary worship often included an altar and the sacrifice of an animal (Genesis 22:6-8, 13).

At Sinai, God gave Moses specific plans for a portable structure to accommodate the wandering nation. The tabernacle was about fifteen feet wide and forty-five feet long. The inner room was called the Holy of Holies or the Most Holy Place. The outer room was called the Holy Place. Surrounding all this was a large courtyard with only one door.

The temple, built later, though much larger, followed this pattern.

Approaching the Most Holy Place, symbolic of God's presence, the worshiper came first to the altar of sacrifice, a symbol of Jesus' crucifixion. Every Old Testament sacrifice previewed the coming sacrifice of the Lamb of God.

God's Purpose Comes Full Circle in Heaven

In the book of Revelation everything God has done to rescue man from sin comes full circle, especially in the last two chapters.

One of the delights of Eden was when God came to His children. Sin destroyed that fellowship (Genesis 3:8), but now, in Heaven, that joy is restored. "The dwelling of God is with man, and he will live with them."

Stone altars upon which lambs were offered, the sacrifices of tabernacle and temple, previewed the day the Lamb of God was offered on the cross.

The Lamb that was slain has become the bridegroom, His apostles the foundation of the city wall. Heaven needs no sacred place, for all is sacred here. There is no temple, no tabernacle, no altar.

Worship in heaven is not going to meet God, for the Lamb and the Lord God Almighty are everywhere here.

The twelve patriarchs of the Old Covenant join with Christ's twelve apostles, each in his own place in God's divine plan.

Even the jeweled foundation stones find their counterpart in the Old Covenant, for they call to mind the richly ornamented breastplate worn by the high priest (Exodus 28:15-30).

Life began in a garden, Eden. Life comes to completion in a garden city.

In the beginning man lost his right to the tree of life; here he has free and open access.

God's first recorded word in creation was "Let there be light." The night of sin descended, and now morning dawns eternally with light for all and forever.

There was no pain in the garden, nor were there tears until man fell. Nor will there be pain in Heaven. The tears of sin have been dried, and by God himself! His redemptive work ends mourning and sorrow.

What Will We Be Like in Heaven?

Have you ever felt left out? That surely has to be one of the worst feelings a person can have.

When I was a boy several of us decided to play a trick on the new boy on the street. Looking back, I am still ashamed that we could be so cruel.

We had been riding our bicycles, and had stopped to catch our breath, when we saw him coming. He had seen us and had hurried to get his bike so he could come and ride with us.

But the deal was that just as he reached where we were, we

For Further Research

Next came the laver, where priests were cleansed by water before entering the tabernacle. Every Christian is a priest, commissioned to offer spiritual sacrifices (1 Peter 2:5; Revelation 1:6).

Within the Holy Place, a picture of the church, stood a large golden lampstand and table spread with twelve loaves of bread changed each Sabbath. These picture the Holy Spirit and the Lord's Supper, giving light and food for our souls, just as the tabernacle had light and food for the body.

Before the Most Holy Place stood an altar of incense, picturing prayer, showing that we approach God through this privileged access.

Between the Holy Place and the Most Holy Place was a veil, through which the high priest went once a year to make atonement.

Christ, our high priest, offered His own blood (Hebrews 9:23-28).

When He died, the temple veil was torn from top to bottom, showing that He has opened the way for us to enter Heaven, where God lives and where we'll be living, too. This is truly the Holy of Holies, the Most Holy Place of all. And the way now is open!

would split in every direction and leave him there. I can still see his disappointment and hurt.

How terrible to feel alone! We'll never know that feeling in Heaven, because God's love will make us welcome (Revelation 21:3). And if we need solitude at times, the vast city will have room for that too.

Heaven will be so satisfying! Here, there's never quite enough time. We're never quite contented. Never quite do our best. Never reach all our goals.

How different in Heaven, freed from the tyranny of the clock and the limitations of the flesh! To be lifted above fatigue and weakness and frustration and disappointment: that will be Heaven!

We'll be with God in Heaven. Instead of going once a week or twice a week or more to a separate place to worship, we will worship God continually.

Nor will it be just by singing songs and saying prayers. Certainly not by sitting on a cloud playing a harp! In Heaven, worship will be opening our hearts to His heart and having His love and our love meet. All the barriers of earth will be gone.

We ought to sigh a little when we think of heaven.
                                        —Gladys M. Hunt[3]

How will we spend all that time? Think of what it will be like to explore Heaven. You'll have a free ticket to everything there. No "Come back later; we're closed." Not in Heaven.

What great good have you always longed for, but never quite realized? You will find it in Heaven.

We'll have the joy of serving our Lord and God. And we won't be embarrassed by failure as we so often are here.

We say we love God, and we do; but our love comes and goes. It isn't always as strong as we want it to be. Sometimes we seem closer to Him than at others. *Self* crowds in, and pushes Him to one side, and we have to ask, "Do we really love Him as we say we do?"

In Heaven we won't have to ask that question, because our love will be cleansed and purified. The city of life will also be the city of love—the highest and holiest love of all.

---

3. Gladys M. Hunt, *Don't Be Afraid to Die* (Grand Rapids, Michigan, Zondervan Publishing House, 1971), p. 58.

Heaven Will Be a Clean City

Sometimes our cities are so dirty. Polluted air, littered streets, uncollected garbage, discarded junk. Heaven will be a clean city, materially clean and spiritually clean. There will be no slums, and there will be no wickedness.

All that hurts, all that brings pain, all that is sinful, all that is deceitful and wrong and shameful will be excluded from Heaven. It wouldn't be Heaven if these things were there.

None was so kind as Jesus and yet
none so stern in His language on hell.
—Herbert Lockyer[4]

When Satan ruined God's creation in the beginning, God promised that the day would come when a woman's child would defeat the devil (Genesis 3:15). That day has come in the city John describes, where:

> The cowardly, the unbelieving, the vile, the murderers, the sexually immoral, those who practice magic arts, the idolaters and all liars—their place will be in the fiery lake of burning sulphur.
>
> —Revelation 21:8

None of these will be in heaven. John wants us to know that, too. It will be quite impossible to take any of our pet sins into the magnificent city. We must be washed in the blood of the Lamb. What if he had kept this from us? What if we didn't know? His warning is clear:

> Nothing impure will ever enter it, nor will anyone who does what is shameful or deceitful, but only those whose names are written in the Lamb's book of life.
>
> —Revelation 21:27

Only those who belong to Jesus will be in Heaven. Only those who have accepted Him as Savior and who serve Him as Lord will

---

4. Herbert Lockyer, *Dying, Death, and Destiny* (Old Tappan, New Jersey, Fleming H. Revell, 1980), p. 72. Used by permission.

be there. It cost God a lot to open Heaven for us. It wasn't cheap; it wasn't easy. Jesus died so we could go there. His cross was the key that unlocked the door.

What do you think? Is all the talk on the tube about the bomb and the arms race and the economy and the Middle East about to put you away? Are you ready to give up on happiness?

Hold on, because the best is on the way, and John has already seen it. It's great!

You're going to live with Jesus forever, in God's house, treated as a son and heir. Life is going to be so good for you that you'll need eternity to savor it.

There's a title deed in Heaven with your name on it. Free. Yours. Jesus paid the bill. He will have it ready for you when you come.

For now, enjoy getting to know Jesus. Live with Him. Spend time with Him in prayer. Let Him come along with you as you run through your day. Get into His Book. Learn everything about Him you can.

The better you know Him here, the more you'll enjoy being with Him there.

LOOK UP
HOLD YOUR HEADS HIGH
FOR YOU WILL SOON BE FREE[5]

Invite someone else to come with you, too. Planet Earth won't be around forever. One of these days we're going to use up our resources. One of these days someone's going to try out the bomb again. One of these days history just might take a sharp turn. So get your friends on the way to Heaven.

No wonder some people look at the future and shudder. They are staring ahead into darkness. They are trying to go it alone. If you don't have Jesus, that's fatal.

Worse than fatal. "Second death," the Bible calls it. Terror. Darkness. Hell. Worse than being incinerated alive. Hopeless. Locked out forever.

Kept out of Heaven because they kept out Jesus from their hearts.

But with Him, the word is Victory! Joy! Excitement! Never-dying happiness; never-ending life.

---

5. Luke 21:28, Philips' Translation.

142

Think of what Heaven will be.

We will be new: "I am making everything new."

We will be able to see: "They will see his face."

We will be able to receive: "He who overcomes will inherit all this."

We will be happy: "No more death or mourning or crying or pain."

We will be free: "On no day will its gates ever be shut."

We will never be afraid: "There will be no night there."

We will be clean: "Nothing impure will ever enter it."

We will be truly and fully alive: "The free gift of the water of life."

We will be active: "His servants will serve him."

We will be comforted: "He will wipe every tear from their eyes."

We will have every need met: "To him who is thirsty I will give to drink without cost from the spring of the water of life."

We will know the Father: "I will be his God and he will be my son."

We will belong: "His name will be on their foreheads."

We will be home: "Now the dwelling of God is with men, and he will live with them. They will be his people, and God himself will be with them and be their God."

And that will be Heaven.

Think It Over

1. How would you describe a sunrise to someone who is blind? Do you see John's problem in trying to describe Heaven to us? You may want to get with a friend and try to describe Heaven to him or her, and have him or her try to tell you what he or she thinks Heaven will be like. Then compare your descriptions with Revelation 21 and 22.

2. For an interesting study, compare the first three chapters in Genesis with these last two chapters in Revelation. Both tell of God's presence, the tree of life, perfection, and of God and His creation being together. Check into it and see what you can find.